BURPEE

AMERICAN GARDENING SERIES

ROCK GARDENING

Charles O. Cresson

PRENTICE HALL GARDENING

New York • London • Toronto • Sydney • Tokyo • Singapore

PRENTICE HALL GENERAL REFERENCE
15 Columbus Circle
New York, New York, 10023

Library of Congress Cataloging-in-Publication Data

Cresson, Charles O.
    Rock gardening / Charles O. Cresson.
        p.   cm.—(Burpee American gardening series)
    Includes index.
    ISBN 0-671-79928-2
    1. Rock gardens.   2. Rock plants.   I. Title.   II. Series.
SB459.C7   1994
635.9'672—dc20   93-12195
                                                        CIP

Designed by Levavi & Levavi

Manufactured in the United States of America

10   9   8   7   6   5   4   3   2   1

First Edition

PHOTO CREDITS: *Agricultural Research Service, USDA:* pp. 92–93; *Armitage, Allan:* pp. 57 top and second from bottom, 60 top and middle left, 61 top and bottom right, 62 top, 64 top and bottom, 65 top left, 66 middle, 67 bottom, 69 bottom, 70 top, 76 middle; *Cresson, Charles:* pp. 16, 20, 57 second from top, 59 top left and top right, 60 bottom left, 65 bottom, 69 top, 73 bottom left, 74 left, 75 both, 81 bottom; *Dirr, Michael:* pp. 9, 12, 19 top, 25, 46 top, 58 left, 63 both, 64 middle, 70 bottom, 71 left, 78 all, 79 all, 80 top left and right, 81 top, 82 bottom left and right, 84 middle, 85 top and middle; *Gevjan, Armen:* pp. 15 left, 39, 66 top, 67 top, 72 top, 73 top; *Grushow, Jane:* pp. 6, 15 right, 19 bottom, 31, 34, 41, 42, 57 bottom, 58 right; *Gyer, John:* pp. 2–3; *Horticultural Photography, Corvallis, OR:* p. 80 bottom; *Mann, Charles:* p. 66 bottom; *Mineo, Baldassare:* pp. 23, 26, 46 bottom, 49, 54, 62 bottom, 72 bottom, 73 bottom right, 82 top, 83 both, 84 top, 85 bottom; *Pavia, Jerry:* p. 71 right; *Pavia, Joanne:* pp. 59 bottom, 84 bottom; *Viette, Andre:* p. 67 middle; *Von Wall, Hermann:* p. 77 top left; *W. Atlee Burpee & Co:* pp. 28 all, 60 bottom right, 61 top left, 65 top right, 68, 74 right, 76 top and bottom, 77 bottom and top right.

Illustrations on pages 32, 35, 36, 37 and 40 by Elayne Sears
Illustrations on pages 86 and 87 by Michael Gale

Acknowledgments

I wish to thank several gardening friends who have contributed generously of their time and experience, in addition to my own long hours of work, to improve this book and its usefulness to gardeners:

Chela Kleiber, former copywriter at Burpee, has kindly given me her personal time to edit my rough drafts, cleaning them up and making numerous improvements. Roxie Gevjan, a tireless rock gardener and seed grower, shared her lifetime of experience with me and was always there in times of need. Baldassare Mineo, of Siskiyou Rare Plant Nursery in Medford, Oregon, also provided extensive technical assistance. Rick Dilworth, of Dilworth Nursery in Oxford, Pennsylvania, has been an invaluable source of information and experience on dwarf conifers. Bob Bartolomei, curator of the Rock Garden at the New York Botanical Garden, has provided experience and inspiration. Joyce Fingerut and Marnie Flook of the American Rock Garden Society shared valuable knowledge and experience. Holly Shimizu of the U.S. Botanical Garden advised me on herbs, particularly thymes. Janet Evans, librarian at The Pennsylvania Horticultural Society, has kindly assisted with the bibliography. Finally, I must thank my editors at Prentice Hall, Rebecca Atwater and Rachel Simon, who always find ways to improve my manuscripts and make the process of writing them so much easier.

On the cover: Purple rock cress, silvery creeping sedum and yellow dwarf wallflowers illustrate the charm of rock gardening in this spring scene.

On preceding page: Natural scenes like this one at Frog Lake, Carson Pass, California, are the inspiration of rock gardeners. Eriogonum umbellatum *(in bloom), sedum and artemesia nestle among the rocks.*

CONTENTS

INTRODUCTION

THE APPEAL OF ROCK GARDENS

Rock gardens are landscapes in miniature, evoking images of the rugged terrain of the world's high mountains. They are inhabited by little plants, many of which hail from above the tree line on those mountaintops, where the climate is harsh and forbidding. Such rigorous climates necessitate dwarf, compact plant forms that can withstand cutting winds, biting cold and blazing sun. Yet, while the size of the plants is reduced, the size of the flowers often is not. High mountain plants are capable of spectacular floral displays out of proportion to the size of the plants.

A rock garden is well suited to the small properties and busy pace of modern life. The small scale of rock garden plants makes them ideal for gardens where space is limited, and a wide range of these plants will fit into a small area where they can be easily tended. Of course, enthusiastic rock gardeners inevitably extend their plantings to create more dramatic scenes and cultivate a great number of their favorite varieties.

Regrettably, rock gardens have the reputation of being labor-intensive. But it is really a matter of scale. These small plants do require care, but when properly treated they can adapt to adverse conditions. Admittedly, there is more work per square foot in a rock garden than in other gardens with larger plants, but arguably not more work per plant. In fact, once it has been established, a rock garden involves less heavy labor. No further tilling, heavy digging or staking is required. Cleanup does not involve volumes of vegetation and compost, and as rock gardens are usually built on a slope or in a raised bed, they are easier to tend than beds at ground level. In fact, getting close enough to care for these little gems is a real joy.

The most effective rock gardens emulate rugged sites in nature. They are inhabited by plants with tough constitutions, whose dwarf scale accentuates the stark, hard quality of the stones they serve to soften. In nature, a wind-swept mountain peak may give way to a rocky cliff or an open slope; at its base sits an alpine meadow or scree (a deep accumulation of stone and gravel with very fast drainage and few nutrients). Whether found in the mountains or simulated in the rock garden, these habitats provide unique microclimates that suit different groups of plants.

Soil is probably the most important factor in growing rock garden plants. Many mountain and rock plants grow in well-drained soils composed of accumulations of stone chips from weathered rock or glacial deposits, mixed with small amounts of organic matter. In fact, many rock plants, adapted to such meager and sterile soils, would be killed by the rich soils of valleys. Rich soil weakens rock plants by stimulating overdrive growth. Stoney mountain soils provide excellent drainage all year, but allow roots to penetrate deeply in search of moisture and nutrients. Almost without exception, drainage and aeration of these rocky soils are the keys to growing rock plants successfully.

Many high elevation plants are familiar to us because they are dwarfed species of popular garden plants from lower elevations. Their tops are more compact to withstand harsh climates, but their root systems are enlarged. Larger root systems anchor the rock plants and penetrate more deeply into cracks and crevices in search of scarce moisture and nutrients. Such familiar plants as yarrow, columbine, *Campanula, Dianthus, Gentian,* poppy and *Veronica* have diminutive relatives suitable for the rock garden.

The terms *alpine, saxatile* and *rock plant* have come to be used almost synonymously, but they are different. Alpine plants come from above the tree line at high elevations. They are especially adapted to cool summer temperatures, a short growing season and a continuous snow cover all winter, which protects plants from severe weather conditions. Saxatile plants grow among rocks, usually in mountainous terrain, but not necessarily in alpine areas. Saxa-

The rugged character of this rock garden showcases the spectacular bloom of dwarf plants at Stonecrop, Cold Springs, NY. A vivid blue gentian is backed by white candytuft (Iberis sempervirens).

tile plants from lower elevations are often easier to grow in low elevation rock gardens than true alpines, particularly in hot climates. *Rock plant* is a general yet meaningful term for the small plants described in this book. Some are alpines, but many are saxatile plants or dwarf plants suitable for a novice's rock garden.

Rock gardens are as diverse as the plants they are designed to contain. In their most rudimentary form, rock gardens are homes for only the easiest and most adaptable dwarf plants. The most complex rock gardens provide a variety of soil types and habitats, including streams, moist bogs and shaded areas. However, most high mountain plants come from open, exposed, dry, rocky situations in full or nearly full sun. This book will discuss these rock plants and the rock garden situations in which they flourish. Once you are familiar with the basics, you may want to include water features or expand the garden into shady areas. Other books in the Burpee American Gardening Series, and other, more detailed books on rock gardening, describe these situations and introduce you to the fascinating plants you can grow in them.

AN HISTORICAL PERSPECTIVE

Rock gardening as we know it today began in the 1920s, so it is a comparatively new manifestation of the art of gardening. Though rockeries were common in Victorian parks of the 19th century, they were not true rock gardens by today's definition. These artificial, gaudy rockeries were often composed of large rocks scattered about the landscape with little regard to the use of plants appropriate to such settings. Nevertheless, innovative rock work and an interest in alpines was emerging.

In 1870, the prolific and an influential English garden writer William Robinson published *Alpine Flowers for the Garden*. He claimed that all alpine plants could be grown in the moderate British climate, a statement that is almost true. Meanwhile, near Geneva, Switzerland, Henry Correvon was pioneering the cultivation and acclimatization of high elevation alpines at lower elevations. His active career as a rock gar-den nurseryman and writer spanned more than 50 years at the turn of the century. His garden, Floraire, in Chene Bourg, can still be visited today. The first of his 37 books was published in 1884. *Rock Garden and Alpine Plants* (1930) was the only one written in English.

In the early 20th century, wealthy hobbyists in Britain created lavish mountain-like rock gardens imitating natural rock formations and grand, artificial peaks. Perhaps the most dramatic example was at Friar Park, near London, where a huge rock garden of 7,000 tons of limestone was topped by a quartz model of the Matterhorn. It even included goat figures on its slopes.

Rock gardening became the rage in Britain in the 1920s. Reginald Farrer became the preeminent spokesman with the publication of his book *My Rock Garden*. He wrote about rock garden construction and dramatic plant collection trips to the mountains of Europe, Burma and China. During the hardships of World War II, Farrer spent long nights writing his greatest work, the two-volume *The English Rock Garden*. It became the first truly definitive work on the subject. Tragically, Farrer died of fever on a plant-collecting trip in the mountains of Burma at the age of 40.

Arguably the finest rock garden to be seen today is at the Edinburgh Botanic Garden in Scotland. Other excellent examples in Great Britain can be found at the Wisley Garden and Kew Gardens, both near London. The popularity of rock gardening continues in England and Scotland and such European countries as Germany and Czechoslovakia. *The Rock Garden and Its Plants* by G. S. Thomas is a fascinating account of the history and evolution of the art.

Rock gardening became pop-

The rock garden at the Edinburgh Botanical Garden in Scotland is one of the finest in the world.

ular in North America in the 1920s, although its popularity lessened during the depression. After the Second World War, interest in rock gardening surged, particularly in the Pacific Northwest, where renewed interest was aroused in part by exposure to Japanese gardens. Asian gardens, based on philosophical and religious concepts, provided Americans with stimulating inspiration for the use of rocks and water in landscapes and rock gardens. European design had been based only on the imitation and romantic interpretation of nature.

George Schenk, a Seattle rock garden nurseryman and designer, was an advocate of the Asian approach in his book, *How to Plan, Establish, and Maintain Rock Gardens* (1964).

The most valuable books are those written by real gardeners with a wealth of personal experience. Northeastern rock gardeners have been particularly prolific. Louise Beebe Wilder gained useful experience for her 1928 book, *Pleasures and Problems of a Rock Garden* in the vicinity of New York City. Doretta Klaber gardened near Philadelphia and published

Rock Garden Plants in 1959. New Jersey nurseryman, Walter Kolaga, produced the highly useful *All About Rock Garden Plants* in 1966.

The most revered rock gardening partnership of the Northeast may well have been the late Lincoln and Laura Louise Foster. Together they wrote and illustrated many articles as well as their instructive book, *Rock Gardening*, in 1968. Their famed garden at Millstream House in northwestern Connecticut no longer exists, but its memory and inspiration live on in photographs and the plant varieties that originated there and now grow in so many other gardens.

Originally, rock gardening in America was most popular in northern regions with cool summers, where traditional rock garden plants and alpines do best. Over the years, however, interest in rock gardening has spread across the country. The concepts remain the same, but the selection of plants varies according to the climate. Most of the plants described in this book are among the most adaptable. A few others, which have more restrictive needs, are mentioned because of their legendary appeal.

American rock gardening has advanced and thrived with the support and enthusiasm of members of the American Rock Garden Society since its founding in 1934. The ARGS remains the best source of information for both amateurs and professionals through regional chapters, publications and local and national meetings. For information, write: Secretary, ARGS, P.O. Box 67, Millwood, NY 10546.

Rock Gardens Open to the Public in North America

Berry Botanic Garden, Portland, OR

Betty Ford Alpine Garden, Vale, CO

Denver Botanical Garden, Denver, CO

Leonard J. Buck Garden, Far Hills, NJ

Montreal Botanic Garden, Montreal, Quebec

New York Botanical Garden, Bronx, NY

Stonecrop, Cold Spring, NY

University of British Columbia Botanic Garden, Vancouver, BC

ROCK GARDENING AS AN ART

Skillful placement of stones in the landscape to create a natural look is an art. Through observation of natural rock formations and geology we can learn how rocks lie, and interpret those observations in our gardens. At the same time, we must consider how the rock features fit into the rest of the garden and landscape for the most appealing effect. A rock feature on a hillside that simulates exposed bedrock is more likely to be attractive than a pile of rocks in the middle of a lawn. But even on a level site, well-designed rock gardens can be made to look natural.

Few people, including experienced gardeners, understand the difference between a rockery and a true rock garden. Proper rock gardening satisfies the unique needs of saxatile plants and makes use of stones to complement them. In extreme cases, all plants not specifically requiring rock garden conditions are excluded. Rockeries involve a less disciplined use of rocks, which are often placed in a haphazard or utilitarian manner in the landscape without regard to examples from nature. Plantings among the rocks often have no particular need of a rock garden environment, and may include such widely adaptable and pedestrian plants as petunias or forsythia, which will grow virtually anywhere.

Many gardeners will be interested in planting a rock garden because it will fit into the landscape as a special feature or solve a problem on a bank such as holding the soil or eliminating mowing. A fortunate few may even have a natural rock feature that can be developed into a garden. Enthusiastic rock gardeners eventually become caught up in growing plants of exquisite beauty and rarity. Most of these require the special soil conditions found in a properly constructed rock garden. Different areas of the rock garden may also be designed to provide the necessary conditions for plants from diverse habitats.

ROCK GARDEN DESIGN

Plant collectors and designers have always been at odds—if not with each other, then within themselves. By *collector* I mean a gardener who is enamored of plants for their beauty and rarity, desiring as many kinds as possible in his collection. (This doesn't refer to collecting from the wild, which should be left to scientists.) By *designer* I mean the artful gardener who creates landscape scenes with stones, land forms and plants. How difficult it is not to allow plants to clutter and overshadow design principles. The establishment of a truly interesting, appropriate and successful community of plants in a design is a challenge for many designers. The finest gardeners have a delicate balance of plant knowledge and innovation.

ROCK GARDENS IN THE LANDSCAPE

Traditional rock gardeners such as Reginald Farrer considered it essential to locate rock gardens in a naturalistic setting, away from formality and man-made structures. He advocated the experience of discovery, as in rounding a bend in a path to encounter a rock garden appearing as a natural feature of the landscape. Today, few of us have large enough properties to isolate our rock gardens. Besides, why not have the garden closer at hand, so that it can be enjoyed in all its beauty throughout the year? Friends of mine have a rock garden built into a bank facing a large picture window. There is something in bloom outside this window almost every month of the year. Such plantings around the house have the added advantage that the dwarf plants will not overgrow the house as so many foundation plants do. Fortunately, the contemporary design of many houses blends comfortably with a naturalistic landscape, of which a rock garden can be an integral part. Only in the case of rectilinear raised beds does formality become a concern of the rock gardener. Every effort must be made to create the illusion that the rocks were placed by the hand of nature.

Due to their limited size and specialized nature, rock gardens need their own space or corner in the landscape; they should occupy a garden "room" or area. Use larger elements such as trees, tall shrubs and hedges to establish a sympathetic setting or background. Many properties have the awkward feature of a bank left from grading or where a driveway has been cut into a hill. This bank is the ideal place for a rock garden or planted wall. It eliminates the need for mowing and provides a profusion of bloom from dwarf plants that will not hang out in the way of the car. Away from the house, the rock garden needs a suitable background. An

This rock garden settles into the slope as it flows across the landscape at Scotland's Edinburgh Botanical Garden. Plants of the same kind are grouped together to provide naturalistic drifts or masses.

informal planting of gradually larger shrubs and perhaps trees should screen it from neighbors and artificial elements. Evergreens are especially useful for year-'round effect.

Most rock gardens are built into slopes, as if they constituted exposed portions of the bedrock beneath. On a level site, it is possible to create the impression of a rock formation jutting up out of the ground, around which a rock garden has been constructed. Its success depends upon the skill with which the stones are placed. The rock formation should not be unnaturally high; instead, it should be low (usually under 2 feet), and spreading. Such rock features can add great character to the design of a garden. A few fortunate gardeners will have an authentic rock feature with which to begin. Devoted rock gardeners

have even been known to search out and purchase properties with such features, regardless of the condition of the house. Most of us, however, must be content to create a successful illusion.

There are advantages to building a rock garden into a slope. This type of garden is generally cheaper to build than other kinds of rock gardens. The problem of drainage has also been solved, although it is essential that the grading channels water away from or around the rock garden and not over it. Water running over the garden can wash out little plants or cover them with mud and silt. Observe runoff during a rain before you begin construction. The top of the slope will be drier, and the bottom will provide a habitat for plants requiring more moisture. A slope or bank of about 45 degrees is

ideal for a rock garden. A very steep, nearly vertical, slope lends itself to a dry retaining wall that can be planted with saxatile plants. A gradual slope is best suited to an alpine meadow.

Most sites can be developed to include a composite of several different kinds of rock garden areas suited to different plants. For instance, the upper areas might include a greater proportion of exposed rocks, crevices for planting and steeper slopes. Further down the slope, soils become deeper and allow more planting space. You might want to include a gravelly scree lower down. Toward the bottom, the grade becomes a gently sloping alpine meadow. Microclimates vary from one side of the rock garden to another (and even around a stone), the northern side being cooler than the southern side.

SOIL CONSIDERATIONS

Although proper soil is one of the most important factors in growing rock plants, it is probably the least important criterion for choosing a site for your rock garden. The native soil is almost never loose enough or well enough drained without modification. During construction you can create the ideal soil mix according to your specifications. Recommended soil mixes for different uses are described in Chapter 2.

The most important consideration in choosing a site is soil drainage. Slopes and raised beds usually allow for good drainage, but rock gar-

dens should not be built in low areas because they tend to flood. Not every rock gardener has the means or inclination to create the ideal soil. Even where the soil is less than ideal, reasonable success is possible on a slope with a surface layer of gravel 2 to 3 inches deep. Although the range of plants will be more limited, the most adaptable rock plants will do quite well. More than anything else, soil determines the kind of rock garden and the plants that can be grown. The general rock garden mix recommended in Chapter 2 will grow a great

many beautiful plants. Many plants, however, have special requirements and need an even faster draining soil or one that is either limey or acidic.

Tree root competition is a soil problem that is difficult to solve permanently, except with a chainsaw through the trunk, because the roots grow back. Tree roots extract nutrients and large amounts of water ·in a short time, necessitating frequent watering and additional feeding. Few rock plants can tolerate the underground competition of these strong roots. Without tree roots, your rock garden will stay moist for long periods and will seldom need watering. Once a rock garden is constructed in the vicinity of trees, roots will begin to grow into it. There is no easy or practical way to remove them. The best way to prevent this is not to construct the garden under the drip line of a tree's branches, but this is not always possible on a small property. It helps to know which trees are the most troublesome. Such deep-rooted trees as oak and hickory are less of a problem, while shallow-rooted trees such as maples, lindens, beeches, poplars, willows and white pines are troublemakers. You can get a fairly accurate assessment by examining the surface roots of a mature tree. A profusion of feeder roots just below the soil or numerous shallow woody roots pushing through the soil surface are signs of shallow roots.

KINDS OF ROCK GARDENS

A scree or talus is the ultimate rock garden habitat for growing difficult species of plants. The essence of a scree is its very well-drained, stoney soil mix, 12 to 18 inches or more deep. In nature, a scree is an accumulation of broken stone and gravel, fast draining and poor in nutrients. They often occur at the bottom of rocky cliffs, so they're not necessarily alpine habitats. Stone chips, grit, sand and a little organic matter accumulate to a considerable depth over many centuries. They are even better drained in the upper level, as the finer particles eventually wash downward. Scree plants need to be tolerant of summer drought. These well-drained, low-nutrient conditions are the secret to preventing the rots common to alpine plants grown in gardens.

Moraines are similar to screes in that they have the same sharply drained, stoney soil, but a film of water flows over the bedrock far below, where deeply penetrating roots pick it up. Plant roots may

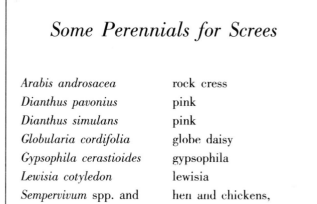

Some Perennials for Screes

Arabis androsacea	rock cress
Dianthus pavonius	pink
Dianthus simulans	pink
Globularia cordifolia	globe daisy
Gypsophila cerastioides	gypsophila
Lewisia cotyledon	lewisia
Sempervivum spp. and hybrids	hen and chickens, houseleek

Penstemon menziesii *grows best in a scree where the gravelly soil provides fast drainage around the roots.*

A scree bed in the rock garden at the New York Botanical Garden in the Bronx.

Some Plants for Alpine Meadows

PERENNIALS

Allium senescens glaucum	flowering onion
Antennaria dioica	pussytoes
Aquilegia flabellata	columbine
Arabis caucasica	rock cress
Dianthus spp. and hybrids	pink
Gentiana septemfida	gentian
Phlox subulata	moss pink
Potentilla aurea	cinquefoil
Pulsatilla vulgaris	pasque flower
Sedum spp. and hybrids	stonecrop
Veronica austriaca teucrium	speedwell

BULBS

Allium oreophilum	flowering onion
Anemone blanda	Greek windflower
Colchicum spp. and hybrids	colchicum, meadow saffron
Crocus spp. and hybrids	crocus
Galanthus nivalis	snowdrop
Iris reticulata	reticulated iris
Narcissus spp. and hybrids	daffodil
Tulipa spp. and hybrids	tulip

SHRUBS

Calluna vulgaris	heather
Daphne cneorum	daphne
Erica carnea	heath
Salix uva-ursi	willow
Spiraea bullata	spirea
Thymus spp. and hybrids	thyme

reach down 15 feet or deeper. The water must be kept moving so it will not become stagnant. In nature, moraines typically occur at the foot of a glacier where water from melting ice flows under the pile of debris deposited by it. In gardens, moraines only need to be a couple of feet deep. Because they are more complicated to construct, they are beyond the scope of this book.

The alpine meadow is a relatively level or gently sloping area where a richer, less sharply drained soil has accumulated, but good drainage is still very important. Though perhaps strewn with rocks, rock features are less prominent. The size of your alpine meadow depends in part on the size of the rock garden as a whole, but as it is a place where bulbs and dwarf plants are often allowed to naturalize, it should not be too cramped. It is best to stick to low plants that will remain in scale, such as low-growing phlox, geraniums, dwarf flowering onions (*Allium*), thyme (*Thymus*), dwarf campanulas, low sedums and dwarf bulbs such as crocus, dwarf daffodils (*Narcissus*) and *Scillas*. Although it is best to exclude turf grasses because they are too vigorous and competitive for most plants, you can suggest an alpine meadow by having a lawn at the bottom of a rock garden that is naturalized with miniature bulbs. Of course, the grass can't be cut until the bulb foliage ripens in late spring or early summer, which means that the rough, natural look is untidy to some gardeners' eyes.

Shady rock gardens are essentially woodland gardens among rocks, often using dwarf plants. Many delightful shade plants are ideally suited to creeping among rocks. Woodland plants prefer soils richer in organic matter that need not be so gravelly and fast draining. They

*This classic interpretation of an alpine meadow at Wisley Garden, in England, is filled with naturalized miniature petticoat daffodils (*Narcissus bulbicodium*) along with dwarf shrubs and the rounded forms of slow-growing cutleaf Japanese maples. It leads to the rock garden in the distance.*

Some Plants for Shady Rock Gardens

PERENNIALS

Anemone nemorosa	European wood anemone
Aquilegia spp. and hybrids	columbine
Aruncus aethusifolius	goatsbeard
Asarum europeum	European ginger
Astilbe simplicifolia	perennial spirea
Carex conica 'Variegata'	sedge
Chrysogonum virginianum	green-and-gold
Dicentra eximia	fringed bleeding heart
Epimedium spp. and hybrids	barrenwort
Hosta spp. and hybrids	plantain lily (dwarf)
Iris cristata	dwarf crested iris
Mitchella repens	partridgeberry
Phlox divaricata	wild sweet William
Phlox stolonifera	creeping phlox
Primula spp. and hybrids	primrose
Sedum nevii	stonecrop
Sedum ternatum	stonecrop
Sempervivum spp. and hybrids	hen and chickens, houseleek
Shortia galacifolia	Oconee-bells
Silene virginica	fire pink
Thalictrum coreanum	meadow rue
Tiarella cordifolia collina	foam flower

FERNS

Asplenium platyneuron	ebony spleenwort
Athyrium filix-femina 'Minutissimum'	dwarf lady fern
Athyrium nipponicum 'Pictum'	Japanese painted fern
Polypodium vulgare	rock cap polypody

SHRUBS

Calluna vulgaris	heather
Cotoneaster spp. and hybrids	cotoneaster
Daphne spp. and hybrids	daphne
Erica spp. and hybrids	heath
Gaultheria procumbens	wintergreen
Hedera helix	English ivy (dwarf varieties)
Ilex crenata	Japanese holly (dwarf varieties)
Paxistima canbyi	paxistima
Picris japonica 'Pygmaea'	lily-of-the-valley bush, andromeda
Rhododendron spp. and hybrids	rhododendrons and azaleas (dwarf)
Vaccinium macrocarpon 'Hamilton'	dwarf cranberry

BULBS

Crocus spp. and hybrids	crocus
Cyclamen spp. and hybrids	cyclamen
Galanthus nivalis	snowdrop
Eranthis hyemalis	winter aconite
Erythronium 'Pagoda'	dogtooth violet
Narcissus spp. and hybrids	daffodil

also prefer an organic mulch such as chopped leaves. The principles and problems of shady rock gardens are so different from sunny rock gardens that the subject is best left to books dealing with shade gardening.

Bogs are acidic and wet, common in alpine areas and at lower elevations at higher latitudes, including New England and Michigan. They form naturally where water collects in a depression and does not flow. Sphagnum moss moves into these wet areas and acidifies the water. Eventually organic matter accumulates, forming peat, because the acidity prevents its decomposition, and a specialized flora becomes established, including various orchids and insectivorous plants. Though true bogs have a decidedly acid soil, in the gardening world the term is often corrupted to mean a wet garden, regardless of the acidity. Bogs are often included in rock gardens in conjunction with a stream or pool, features covered in another book in The Burpee American Gardening Series, *Water Gardening*, and also in more advanced rock garden books.

Paths and steps are a necessary part of all but the smallest rock gardens. Little plants cannot be admired or cared for without getting close to them. The necessity of paths does not mean they must be unattractive or utilitarian. The charm of rock garden paths is that stray seedlings and creeping plants from adjacent beds will make their way onto the paths. Paths make an excellent seed bed from which you can transplant or give away young plants, but don't clean them all out. Encourage low-growing varieties to take up permanent residence wherever traffic permits around the edges and between the stones. These plants serve to soften and visually knit the path into the rest of the garden. Low or creeping plants make good permanent residents along the edge and between the stones. Creeping thymes tolerate some foot traffic and emit a pleasant fragrance when bruised, as does Corsican mint (*Mentha requienii*). For planted paths, include soil in the foundation for nourishment instead of just gravel or sand.

The planted wall is the ideal spot to grow many fine saxatile plants. Saxatiles delight in the perfect drainage that this vertical "bed" provides, and they enjoy being wedged in between the rocks. The kind of wall required is called a "dry" wall, meaning that it is constructed without mortar. It is filled behind with a gravelly rock garden soil. The plants grow between the stones. If the wall

Some Plants for Planting in Paths

Achillea ageratifolia	yarrow
Antennaria dioica	pussytoes
Dianthus deltoides	maiden pink
Mentha requienii	Corsican mint
Sedum spp., low types	stonecrop
Thymus spp.	thyme

Some Plants for Planting in Walls

Aethionema 'Warley Rose'	stone cress
Arabis procurrens	rock cress
Arabis sturii	rock cress
Aubrieta deltoidea	aubretia
Aurinia saxatilis	basket-of-gold
Campanula portenschlagiana	bell flower
C. poscharskyana	bell flower
Dianthus spp.	pink
Gypsophila repens	creeping gypsophila
Hypericum olympicum	St.-John's-wort
Iberis sempervirens	candytuft
Phlox subulata	moss pink
Potentilla tridentata	three-toothed cinquefoil
Saponaria ocymoides	soapwort
Sedum sieboldii	stonecrop
Sempervivum spp.	hen and chickens, houseleek
Thymus spp.	thyme

holds back the soil in a bank, it is called a retaining wall. A properly constructed dry retaining wall will last a lifetime, perhaps even outlasting a wall with cement between the stones. Dry walls are easy to build (see pages 39–40).

Alpines and saxatile plants don't actually need stone to be healthy. As long as their needs for good drainage, air circulation and light are provided, they will do just fine. In regions where stone is scarce, rock gardeners often grow their plants in raised beds and troughs. Raised beds provide ideal conditions in which to grow rock plants. Being elevated above the surrounding area protects tiny plants from the clumsy feet of dogs and people, and brings the plants closer to eye level. Elevation provides perfect drainage in a bed filled with the appropriate soil mix. The soil may be held in place by stone walls or even treated wood, although the wood is less attractive. Provided they are not too wide, all parts of elevated beds are easily reached, even by gardeners in wheelchairs.

Unfortunately, raised beds are not always a satisfying element in the landscape, where they can appear awkward. Try to tie them into something else or make them an essential element of the design. For instance, locate one where it helps to define a space, much as a low hedge would, or locate it in front of a bank or shrub planting. A raised bed might also serve as a central focal point, fulfilling a function similar to that of a low coffee table in the middle of a room.

A beautifully planted wall at the Edinburgh Botanical Garden, Scotland. This is actually a raised bed, surrounded on all sides by the wall.

This raised bed, in the form of a mound, blends easily with its surroundings.

*Troughs are an ideal way to grow dwarf rock and alpine plants, Tufa rocks in the trough
give the impression of a miniature landscape. Moss pink (Phlox) grows at the corners
with white rockfoil (Saxifraga) behind. Authentic stone troughs such as this one are scarce,
but those made from "hypertufa" are popular substitutes.*

Troughs or stone sinks often provide the most suitable homes for very small rock plants. In fact, many will grow better in these containers than in the open ground. The soil and drainage in each can be specially adapted, and the mobility of a trough enables placement in the ideal exposure for the needs of the inhabitants. The practice of planting alpines in old stone farm watering sinks began in England about 1925. Such containers are scarce enough in England, and practically unobtainable here. Fortunately, suitable substitutes are easily made from a cement, perlite and peat mixture called *hypertufa* (see pages 40–41). Not only are they more available (because you can make them), they are lighter in weight and easier to handle. Hypertufa even weathers like real stone. Other less attractive but serviceable substitutes can be found, such as Styrofoam boxes that have been painted gray.

Troughs should be kept outdoors for as much of the year as possible, though in harsh climates they must be given protection during the winter, as described in Chapter 3. Troughs are an extremely rewarding facet of rock gardening, but they require more regular care than plants in the open ground, particularly when it comes to watering.

SCALE

Effective use of scale and perspective are especially important in rock garden design. We wish to evoke images of a rugged terrain by making use of wee plants, which are often surrounded by the apparent contradiction of large trees in a comparatively small space. Use the largest stones possible in all cases to help establish their dominance. Using numerous small stones is no substitute for size. The number of stones depends on the design. Stones should also vary in size and spacing, sometimes touching each other. Several large rocks should be accompanied by smaller ones. Choose plants according to the size of the gar-

Some Plants for Troughs

PERENNIALS

Aethionema 'Warley Rose'	stone cress
Antennaria dioica 'Nye-wood Variety'	pussytoes
Aquilegia bertolonii	columbine
Arabis androsacea	rock cress
Arabis sturii	rock cress
Aurinia saxatilis 'Tom Thumb'	basket-of-gold
Dianthus pavonius	pink
Dianthus simulans	pink
Geranium dalmaticum	hardy geranium
Gypsophila cerastoides	gypsophila
Lewisia cotyledon	lewisia
Mentha requienii	Corsican mint
Primula auricula	primrose, auricula
Saxifraga paniculata	rockfoil
Sedum dasyphyllum	stonecrop
Sempervivum spp. and hybrids	hen and chickens, houseleek
Solidago virgaurea minutissima	goldenrod

SHRUBS

Cotoneaster microphyllus thymifolius	cotoneaster
Daphne cneorum	daphne
Genista dalmatica	hardy geranium
Ilex crenata 'Rock Garden'	Japanese holly
Salix uva-ursi	willow
Salix yesoalpina	willow
Thymus spp. and hybrids	thyme

CONIFERS

Juniperus communis 'Compressa'	juniper
Picea abies 'Weiss'	dwarf Norway spruce
Picea glauca 'Pixie'	dwarf white spruce
Tsuga canadensis 'Cole'	dwarf weeping hemlock

BULBS

Allium oreophilum	flowering onion
Crocus spp. and hybrids	crocus

den. An expansive rock garden can accommodate plants of greater size, while plants in a smaller space, among small stones, should be very dwarf.

Illusions of distance and scale can be created by the use of size and color. Although smaller plants may make stones look larger and further away, they should be planted in masses that have sufficient impact from a distance. Soft colors also appear to be further off, while bright colors seem closer. Small plantings need to be kept close at hand to be fully appreciated.

I advise beginning rock gardeners to start small and expand later. Many home owners have small rock gardens, due to limited time and the size of their properties. For this reason, most of the plants in this book are comparatively dwarf varieties, suited to the scale of small gardens.

PLANTS FOR THE ROCK GARDEN

For many rock gardeners the main attraction is the vast array of plants that can be grown and the challenge of growing them successfully. Purists insist that only those plants requiring specific rock garden conditions should be included in those special environs. Others allow themselves to include dwarf plants that are in keeping with the spirit and scale of the mountain environment. Size is also an important qualification. A general rule is that annuals and perennials should be smaller than 1 foot in height and shrubs should be under 3 feet. Of course, it is necessary to choose plants that can grow in your climate. Some plants are much easier to grow than others, and have a wide adaptability in many regions.

Strictly speaking, alpines are plants that grow naturally above the tree line in the various mountain ranges of the world. In reality, rock gardeners tend to use the term to describe any small mountain plant. True alpines come from a lean, harsh environment where summers are bright but cool, and the growing season is short. Winters are long and very cold, but the plants are continuously covered with a protective layer of snow. Not only does the snow provide insulation from the cold, but it also prevents dehydration from wind and sun. At the same time it keeps the plants dry, as there is no free moisture.

Alpine plants have adapted to these conditions with reduced, compact, tufted or bunlike (sometimes hard to the touch) forms that deflect wind. The leaves are small, narrow, cylindrical or needlelike to reduce the surface area and dehydration. Some have hairs on their foliage to protect leaf surfaces from harsh sun, deflect wind and hold moisture. Root systems are larger and deeper than their low elevation counterparts. Water may be many feet below the surface during dry seasons and these small plants need to resist uprooting in harsh weather. These adaptations, which are geared to retaining moisture, can cause problems in many low elevation gardens. Both heat and moisture (including humidity) can cause stress, which increases susceptibility to various rot diseases. Consequently, drainage and air circulation are critical. Moisture is also a problem during the winter. Winters without snow cover can be too wet and promote root and crown rots in soils without perfect drainage.

If it weren't for the spectacular floral displays of these fussy alpines, gardeners would be content to pass them up. But alpines have adapted to harsh environments by not compromising on their reproductive capabilities. Pollinators can be scarce in high mountain climates. With unreliable weather conditions and a short growing season, these plants can't afford to waste time attracting insects. Usually their disproportionately large flowers, remarkable for their delicacy and range of color, come all at once in a burst. Some of the most beautiful pastel-colored varieties are the mossy saxifrages that are so difficult to grow.

Saxatile plants are not true alpines, but they do require the dry, well-drained conditions found among rocks. They are usually less compact and more often form low mats of foliage, such as moss pink (*Phlox subulata*). Saxatile plants from lower elevations are often easier to grow than true alpines, and make fine rock garden subjects. They too may be native to dry, open habitats, and may have difficulty surviving hot, muggy midsummers unscathed.

Many rock plants are perennials: hardy plants that don't produce woody stems. Some

Some Easy Plants Adapted to Many Regions

Achillea tomentosa	yarrow
Aethionema 'Warley Rose'	stone cress
Armeria juniperifolia	thrift, sea pink
Aurinia saxatilis	basket-of-gold
Cotoneaster microphyllus thymifolius	cotoneaster
Dianthus caesius	Cheddar pink
Genista pilosa	broom
Geranium cinereum	cranesbill
Gypsophila repens	gypsophila
Iberis sempervirens 'Little Gem'	candytuft
Juniperus procumbens 'Nana'	creeping juniper
Phlox subulata	moss pink
Saponaria ocymoides	soapwort
Sedum cauticola	stonecrop
Thymus praecox arcticus	thyme

perennials, such as campanulas, die back to the ground each winter. Many rock plants are also evergreen, maintaining their compact forms all through the winter. *Lewisia cotyledon*, candytufts (*Iberis*), and moss pinks (*Phlox subulata*) are all evergreens.

Annuals are also suitable for the rock garden, if they are small enough to coexist with their diminutive neighbors without crowding them out. Such self-sowing annuals as alpine poppy must be weeded out where they seed into other plants, but they are otherwise of suitable size.

Many varieties of small bulbs are ideal companions for rock garden plants. Crocus, both spring and autumn flowering, and dwarf tulips are among my favorites. Beware of bulbs that develop large foliage after they bloom. I use them but find that they must not be planted close to small plants that may be overshadowed. Dwarf daffodils, such as 'Tête-à-Tête', and dwarf iris (*Iris reticulata*) are short when in flower, but the foliage soon elongates considerably. In autumn, colchicum bears flowers without unwieldy foliage, but in spring large foliage emerges, requiring a good deal of space from March until it dies in June. Some of the small bulbs that would seem to make good rock garden subjects seed alarmingly and may become weed problems. It is best to avoid Siberian squill (*Scilla sibirica*), glory-of-the-snow (*Chionodoxa* spp.) and *Puschkinia*. Let them seed and grow vigorously elsewhere in your garden.

Woody plants are essential elements in the rock garden, providing height and contrasting forms. Though few dwarf shrubs or dwarf conifers are true alpines, they suggest the effect of trees and shrubs dwarfed by the rigors of mountain climates. Since they are larger than other plants, they must be used sparingly to avoid crowding and destroying the sense of proportion. In all but the largest rock gardens, only woody plants under 3 feet in height should be used.

Dwarf shrubs may be deciduous or evergreen and most also have attractive flowers. Daphnes have particularly fragrant flowers, and lavender has aromatic foliage as well as fragrant flowers. The foliage of some dwarf rhododendrons takes on an attractive purplish tint during the winter. Japanese holly has insignificant flowers but the deep green evergreen foliage is a major asset. Nearly all dwarf conifers are evergreen and offer a wide range of shapes, sizes and foliage colors, including deep green, light green, blue-green and gold.

"Dwarf" is a vague and relative term, particularly with conifers. Dwarf conifers are slow growing compared to the full-sized species from which they originated, but they can still reach great size, given enough time. As many rock gardeners have discovered, they outgrow their allotted space sooner or later. Consequently, the dwarf conifers recommended in this book are some of the slowest-growing kinds.

Even the slowest-growing dwarf conifers may revert or mutate to faster-growing forms. Usually this becomes evident when a single branch begins to shoot out faster than the rest of the plant. If allowed to continue, the reversion will take over and your plant will grow into a tree.

Dwarf conifers in this rock garden provide accents and simulate trees that are dwarfed by harsh alpine conditions. Although slow growing, they will eventually become too large, out of scale and need to be replaced. This rock garden is built with tufa stone which creates an ideal environment for many difficult-to-grow rock plants.

Another kind of reversion is a branch that changes its foliage shape or color. Reversions should be cut off as soon as noticed to preserve the parent plant. As an experiment, you may want to root as cuttings the branches you have removed to see what kind of plant they become on their own.

Wherever you garden, the climate will dictate the kinds of plants that you can grow, restricting some, providing opportunities to grow others. Southern gardeners will have great difficulty with many alpines, but less cold-hardy, heat-tolerant plants that are unsuitable for northern climates will make admirable substitutes. The best way to discover the appropriate plants for your climate is to learn from local rock gardeners. The best way to meet them is by joining your local chapter of the American Rock Garden Society (see page 91).

DESIGNING ROCK GARDEN PLANTINGS

Placement of plants in a rock garden is a matter of personal taste and aesthetics. As with any discipline, however, certain elements of style and convention have developed over the years that help adherents achieve the objectives of a naturalistic planting. Initially it may be difficult to think in terms of plant combinations when the plants themselves are unfamiliar. In such a case you can begin with the satisfaction of just growing them and getting acquainted. In time you'll form ideas and make changes.

The traditional approach has been to plant the tiniest plants at the highest point, to symbolize alpines above the tree line, with taller plants lower down the slope. This works fine in a monolithic rock garden. In a small garden it is impractical, and it usually makes more sense to place the small plants toward the front where they are most easily seen and appreciated. Even this is not a hard and fast rule, because most plants in the rock garden will be small and not likely to block the view beyond. Tall forms, such as a dwarf conifer, interspersed among lower forms, make a very interesting scene.

Use height and form as design elements to provide contrasts and accents.

The planting design depends in part on the size of the rock garden. Large rock gardens require the use of some larger plants for scale. Small plants must be massed in groups to achieve visual impact. These masses should be a single variety, either of a single color or a blend of colors, among seedlings of the same type, as they would be found wild in a colony. When grouping plants, use an irregular pattern for a natural effect. Use vigorous, mat-forming plants to keep peripheral areas of large rock gardens under control with reduced maintenance.

Vigorous varieties are useful but can overrun more delicate species. They must be kept apart if you, the gardener, do not want to become a constant policeman. Confine the delicate beauties to the company of others with like strength and vigor. Planting them in a crevice between large rocks is another way to isolate them from rambunctious neighbors.

There is no rule mandating that rock garden plantings should achieve complete coverage of the surface. In fact, in harsh climates or on poor soils, rock plants are often widely spaced, each one an isolated specimen. In the garden, it is best to space them far enough apart so that they have room to mature without growing together. This promotes their well-being through good air circulation, and reduced competition for nutrients, water and light. The situation is somewhat different in an alpine meadow, where richer soil supports a lusher community of species crowded in together.

The great majority of rock plants bloom in spring, but with careful selection your floral display can continue through the summer into fall, and even during winter in many climates. Whatever the season, even a few blooms will enhance a successful design.

Flowers are but one facet of the seasonal beauty of rock gardens. Other important factors to consider are foliage color and texture, plant forms and interesting stones. Though conifers do not bloom, they present a rich array of colors from the deepest greens to bright gold, blue and gray. Moreover, evergreen conifers,

Large sweeps of a single variety are most effective in this large heather garden.

shrubs and perennials maintain a presence in the garden throughout the year. The foliage of many of these changes color with the seasons. Some evergreen rhododendrons and conifers deepen to purple in winter. Such wintergreen bulbs as *Sternbergia lutea* are summer dormant but send up their foliage (with yellow flowers) in autumn to last through the winter until the following spring. Even deciduous perennials may hold up their dried seedheads through the winter. Plant form, foliage texture and color vary dramatically from one plant to another. Striking ever-green rosettes of hen and chickens (*Sempervivum*) come in all sizes with foliage colors of green, reddish or even silver. Moss pink (*Phlox subulata*) forms a mat of fine-textured needlelike foliage. Dwarf conifers are available in low, flat forms, rounded forms, irregular forms and upright spiky forms. With such choices, the potential for combining plants with similar bloom seasons or complementary foliage is endless. It is especially rewarding to create a plant combination that plays off the color and texture of the stones nearby.

Make the design process easier by doing it in an orderly fashion. Begin with the largest, most permanent plants first and work down to the smallest, least permanent. First decide where to put a few crucial evergreen shrubs or conifers. Establish a rhythm or flow. Add deciduous shrubs. Then work around these with evergreen perennials, followed by deciduous perennials, which have less of a presence in winter. Finally add spring and fall bulbs that are relatively small and have long periods of dormancy. Not only should you think about the design in this order, but you should plant in this order, too.

BUILDING YOUR ROCK GARDEN

Understand the materials that make up a rock garden before you begin to build it. This chapter discusses soils, stone and the different ways to put them together. Proper construction is the hardest part, but the benefits will last a lifetime.

SOILS

Soil type is a controllable factor and, in fact, getting the soil "right" is far more important than the presence of rocks. A desirable rock garden soil consists of good topsoil or loam with enough sand or grit mixed in to keep it open and well drained. "Open" means that there is lots of pore space for aeration and to let excess water drain away rapidly.

Soil acidity and alkalinity are measured as pH on a scale of 1 to 14. A pH of 7 is neutral. A low, acid pH falls below 7. A high, alkaline (or basic) pH reads above 7. Soil acidity is more critical to some plants than others. The nearly neutral range of 6.5 to 6.8 will satisfy the greatest number of plants. Calcifuge plants, such as rhododendrons, azaleas, heathers and many woodland plants, require an acid soil between 4.0 and 5.5. They cannot tolerate lime in the soil. Calcicole plants prefer or require lime in the soil (7.0 to 7.5). *Dianthus* and *Gypsophila* grow best in a soil with lime, although they are adaptable and can live without it in a moderately acidic or neutral soil. The best time to adjust soil pH is at the time of mixing. Add pulverized limestone or limestone chips to raise the pH. (Hydrated lime is not suitable because it may burn and its effects are short-lived.) Acid peat moss or leaf mold from oaks and conifers lowers pH. You have a greater chance of successfully changing an acid soil to an alkaline one than the reverse, so if you want an acid soil don't start with an alkaline topsoil. If in doubt about the kind of soil you need, don't add lime. You can always add it later, but you cannot remove it.

It is always advisable to have your soil tested so you know what the pH is at the beginning. The cooperative extension service of most state universities offers this service. You can purchase a special envelope at a garden center, follow simple directions and mail in a sample of your soil. For more information ask at your local nursery, garden center or cooperative extension service. The test will tell you how much of which amendment to add. Soils are inclined to return to their original pH with time and should be tested and adjusted periodically. Rock gardeners have a different concept of soil

Built into a slope, this rock garden is a fitting feature of a home landscape.

fertility than do perennial and vegetable gardeners. Most rock plants have adapted to moderate-to-low fertility, which suits their tempered vigor. As mountain plants, they resent the rich soils of valleys, but they will not thrive if starved. Use manure and fertilizers with care.

Before you build your rock garden, decide on the kinds of plants you wish to grow and choose a soil mix to suit them. If you are not quite sure what kind of soil you need, the Basic Rock Garden Soil Mix on page 29 will support the widest range of plants if the pH is adjusted to fall in the range of 6.2 and 7.5. For the greatest diversity of plants, you can construct your garden so that different sections of the rock garden have different kinds of soil.

Soil Components

Heavy clay soils are composed largely of very fine (microscopic) particles that pack down and dry to a concrete-like hardness. Because these tiny particles hold nutrients, clay soils are very fertile. Sandy soils are made up mostly of large, sandlike particles. They are very well-drained, rather infertile and don't pack hard. Loam is a general term referring to a particularly good topsoil that is easy to work, fertile and does not pack down readily. Loam is the best soil to use in your mixes. If all you have is clay, use half as much, and make up the difference with extra sand or grit.

Drainage materials are essential to loosen soils for air and moisture penetration. The larger the particles, the better they accomplish this objective. Sand's fine particles may be too small for the job. When sand is called for (e.g., in seed mixes), be sure to use a coarse sand, which is sold as sharp or concrete sand. This sand has a higher percentage of larger particles in it. Finishing or builder's sand is a grade finer, and is not satisfactory for a rock garden mix. Beach sand is even finer, and should never be used. The next larger-particle-sized material above sand is called chicken or turkey grit (from agricultural feed stores). It varies slightly in size, but is about three times the size of granulated sugar. A similar product sold in the mid-Atlantic states is traction grit (also sold as filter sand) which is $2/16$-to $3/16$-inch in size. You may also find it in the winter in lumberyards and home centers because it is used when a car gets stuck in ice or snow. Traction grit is a silica sand with a nearly neutral pH. It is always best to check the composition of the grits to determine whether they are from limestone, sandstone or granite, which will affect the pH of your soil.

Gravel and crushed stone are virtually synonymous terms for the coarsest drainage materials. Besides promoting drainage, gravel effectively discourages rodents from digging, tunnelling, undermining rocks and eating your plants. The more gravel you have in the soil, the better the gravel will work to repel these pests. Gravels are sifted or washed for size, and the finest "screenings" or "sift-

ings" are sifted out (make sure that you don't get any of the fine siftings).

You can mix gravel into the soil, or use it as a mulch on top of the soil. The best size of gravel for rock gardens is $3/8$ or $3/4$ inch. This is perhaps the most difficult size to find at quarries because it has limited use for other purposes. You will find that different kinds of stone make different kinds of gravel. Granite is hard, slightly acidic and nonabsorbent. Limestone absorbs and holds water, and is alkaline in reaction. More about stone shortly.

The best drainage material is the hardest to get. It is a porous fired clay, broken in pieces (sort of like crushed flower pot shards). It holds an extraordinary amount of water that can be used by the plants during dry spells without interfering with drainage and aeration. You may have to search long and hard for it. A current brand name is "Turface." It is used on golf courses and is available from turf and golf course supply companies.

Finding a suitable drainage material is not easy and you may have to do a bit of searching. The products vary according to region and the native stone from which they are quarried. The terminology varies, too. Local quarry representatives will be helpful, but you can be sure that unless they are true rock gardeners (which is about as likely as finding palms on the Matterhorn) they are not likely to understand your needs. Take my word for it: you'll have to explain exactly what you want.

Clay soil

Sandy soil

Loamy soil

Organic matter is an important component of all soils. The decomposed remains of plants and animals, it contains valuable nutrients that are slowly released to the plants as needed. Compost, leaf mold and peat are similar, and for the most part, interchangeable, in rock garden soil mixes, with a few differences. You make garden compost yourself from grass clippings, prunings, vegetable scraps and general yard waste. Garden compost generally has a neutral pH and is rich in nutrients. It may be too rich for many rock plants when used alone. Leaf mold is essentially rotted tree leaves. It should be decomposed to the point of being dark and crumbly with few identifiable leaves remaining. It is an excellent source of slow-release nutrients, but is not as rich as garden compost. The acidity of leaf mold depends on the kind of leaves from which it is derived. Oak leaves and conifer needles make an acid leaf mold, while leaf mold from most other leaves is close to neutral.

Both compost and leaf mold are free. But you have to buy peat, and there are several kinds. Canadian sphagnum peat moss is light brown, coarsely fibrous, acidic (pH 3.4 to 4.8) and virtually lacking in nutrients. It is, however, an excellent soil conditioner, and ideal for acid-loving plants. For the few years until peat moss breaks down, it is also very moisture retentive. Sedge peat, while a little more nutritious, is finer in texture, not as moisture retentive and breaks down faster.

Leaf mold is probably the best source of organic matter for soil mixes. The richness of compost can be offset by combining it with peat moss. If you cannot obtain either leaf mold or compost, use peat moss alone with a couple of handfuls of dried manure per bushel of mix. While this isn't very precise, it works.

Soil Mixes

The following formulas are general, and can be modified as needed, depending on the materials available and your climate. (Experienced rock gardeners debate the virtues of their own formulas.) The damper the climate, the better-drained the mix needs to be, and the more crushed stone will be needed. In drier climates, more soil should be added and sand should be used in place of crushed stone.

BASIC ROCK GARDEN SOIL MIX

1 part loamy topsoil
1 part crushed stone (or grit or sharp sand)
1 part leaf mold (or compost or peat)

Modifications:
If using peat moss:
To neutralize acidity, add 1 cup pulverized limestone per bushel of mix
To add nutrients, add 1 cup dried manure or ½ cup 5-10-5 fertilizer per bushel of mix

GRITTY LIME SOIL MIX

1 part loam
1 part leaf mold (or compost or peat)
1 part crushed stone (or grit or sharp sand)
½ part crushed limestone (⅜–¾") or crushed seashells

ACID SOIL MIX

1 part acid loam
1–2 parts peat (enrich peat as above) or acid leaf mold (e.g., from conifer needles or oak leaves)
1 part sharp sand (or grit or crushed stone)

SCREE SOIL MIX

3 parts stone chips
1 part sharp sand
1 part leaf mold (or compost or peat)
(½ part loam, optional)

Mixing Large Quantities of Soil the Easy Way

It is far easier to mix soil separately and then bring it in to fill the rock garden as you build than to mix it on the site. The easiest place to mix soil is on a paved surface, such as a driveway. Measure and pile the ingredients to one side of the pavement in layers. Using a flat-bottomed shovel, scoop the soil from the bottom of the pile and move it to a new pile. Dump each shovelful of soil on the top of the new pile and let it run down the sides. This layering mixes the ingredients without your having to turn them. Return the pile to the original location using the same technique. The soil will be thoroughly mixed.

MULCH

Mulch is any material placed on top of the soil. In rock gardening, it is usually crushed stone or gravel, although in some cases it is organic, as in the case of shredded leaves or bark. Mulch is usually preferable to bare soil. Mulch keeps the soil moist and moderates its temperature, keeping it cool in summer and warm in winter. Mulch also helps to supress weeds. Because it covers the soil, it prevents rain from splashing mud onto small plants, which is unsightly and can even kill them. Mulches also provide an attractive background for your plants. For this reason the color of your mulch is important. Gravel mulches should match the stone in color; for example, use gray gravel mulch with gray stone and brown gravel with brown stone. Then they will appear to be derived from the same geologic source.

A stone mulch has special benefits for rock plants and is essential to their well-being in moist climates. A crushed-stone mulch drains water away from the delicate crowns of the plants and provides a dry surface for foliage to rest upon, which prevents disease. Crushed stone is also devoid of many of the harmful disease organisms found in moist soil, further reducing the opportunities for infection. It even helps to discourage slugs from eating your plants. Use the same size (⅜- to ¾-inch) crushed stone or gravel as recommended for the soil mixes, and apply it up to 2 inches deep. Once applied, stone mulches effectively hold the surface of the soil in place, and are even more stable when held in place by plants.

Organic mulches may be used in shaded rock gardens or woodland gardens, and are ideal for such plants as rhododendrons. They provide organic matter that enriches the soil as they decompose. Leaves make the best organic mulch because they are nutritious and feed plants slowly as they break down. They also have the advantage of being readily available from overhead trees (free of charge). To avoid smothering small plants, it is best to shred leaves before using them as mulch. You can get away without shredding leaves if they are small and do not mat down. Such large, soft leaves as maple, sycamore and magnolia must be shredded or they will mat and prevent moisture from reaching the soil. Other organic mulches are shredded bark and finely ground wood chips. These are attractive, but have little nutritional value.

STONE

When you have observed stone and natural rock formations a little, you will begin to develop an understanding of how to use stone in your rock garden. There are many different kinds of stone, each with different properties that affect its suitability for various uses and plants. As a gardener, you will learn to look at the characteristics of color, hardness, shape and strata (layers) in stone.

Flat and blocky stone is easier to build walls with, but stone with interesting shapes makes more interesting rock gardens. Rounded boulders are difficult to build with because they don't fit together well. In a rock garden they do not suggest an affinity to each other or an underground connection, as stones with shape and strata might. They lack the character of cracks, crevices and angles, but will enhance the effect of a rock-strewn alpine meadow, seeming to have been dropped there by an ancient glacier. In fact, such boulders are commonly found in glaciated areas such as New England. Rounded river stones present similar problems to the boulders but are useful, along with pebbles, in simulated dry streambeds.

Very hard stone will last indefinitely, but it is more difficult to shape or break to make it fit a tight spot. Very soft stone may weather too easily and may even disintegrate over a period of years, as happened in a 20-year-old wall of mine. Hardness is also related to a stone's ability to absorb and store water. Soft, porous stone can absorb remarkable quantities of water, which is then made available to plant roots in times of drought. You can get an idea of a stone's porosity by

Tufa is highly prized by rock gardeners. Its porosity allows plants to be planted directly into the stone, a location which many difficult-to-grow plants prefer. The flower in bloom on the large rock is Erodium chamaedryoides.

observing the amount of moss or algae on its surface after it has been sitting out in the elements for a while. Moisture retentive stone is not essential, but it can definitely be helpful in hot, dry climates.

Old stone from woods and fields is valued for its soft, weathered surface that lends an established appearance to a rock garden. It is also more expensive. The sharp edges of freshly quarried stone wouldn't normally be found exposed in nature. You can hasten the weathering of some stone by applying milk, buttermilk or manure tea to the surface. Manure tea is an old-fashioned fertilizer made by soaking a burlap bag of manure (usually cow) in water for several days. Apparently these liquids supply nutrients that encourage the growth of algae and mosses.

Types of Stone

Stone can be classified by the way it was formed. Igneous rock, such as granite and basalt, was formed by lava that cooled relatively rapidly. It is very hard with little visible strata, and does not absorb water. Sedimentary rock was formed from mineral debris that accumulated and hardened, often on the ocean floor, as evidenced by fossilized shells. It is typified by prominent strata and varies in hardness, but it usually absorbs water readily. Limestone and sandstone, which are sedimentary rocks, are well suited for use in rock gardens. Metamorphic rock has been changed by the effects of heat and pressure. Gneiss is transformed granite, slate comes from shale and marble from limestone.

Some Common Stone for Rock Gardens

Granite—*very hard igneous (or metamorphic) rock with a fine grain, white to gray or pink to reddish, impervious to roots and moisture. Surface does not weather significantly. One of the least desirable for rock gardens.*

Basalt—*hard, fine-grained igneous rock similar to granite, dark gray or brownish gray to black, not water absorbent, but weathers slightly more readily than granite.*

Gneiss—*coarse-textured, layered metamorphic rock, usually dark gray, often banded with white. Slightly softer than granite, but not very water absorbent.*

Sandstone—*sedimentary rock, light tan to warm pinkish brown or red, hardness varies, but the surface weathers attractively with time in the garden. Porous enough to hold moisture, nearly neutral pH, suitable for a wide range of plants.*

Limestone—*sedimentary rock, white to gray and buff or less commonly black or red; porous and weathers well. Hardness varies, but generally soft. Leaches some lime, but this is tolerated by most plants, even by acid lovers if a good acid soil is on top of it.*

Tufa—*a limestone mostly found in caves where it is deposited by dripping water. So porous that plants readily root into it and extract moisture. Soft at first, but hardens when exposed to the elements. Highly valued by rock gardeners, but difficult to obtain.*

Shale—*soft, layered sedimentary rock that splits easily. Somewhat absorbent. Yellow to red, gray-green, black. May be brittle.*

Schist—*metamorphic rock, variable white, gray to greenish, reddish or black. May be brittle with flaky layers, often with tiny reflective pieces of mica, depending on type. Very absorbent, but its irregular, lumpy shape makes it difficult to use.*

Obtaining Stone

Few gardeners are fortunate enough to have a supply of natural stone on their property. Most of us have to settle for purchasing stone from a quarry. It is usually sold by the ton, though occasionally by the pound to home owners. If you have access to a truck, it is cheaper to pick it up yourself and save the cost of delivery. Here's how it works: You drive your truck in and it is weighed empty. After loading, it is weighed again and you pay for the difference. Taking your own truck is usually the only way to enjoy the advantage of hand-picking your own stone. This is actually quite important, because in a rock garden every stone counts. Some quarries won't allow hand-picking under any circumstances, for insurance reasons. Still, it pays to ask, and you will have a better response if you show up dressed to work, with heavy work shoes and gloves.

Not all quarries are "working" quarries, that is, blasting out their own stone. If they are, you will probably have a choice between their own stone and several other kinds of stone brought in from elsewhere on pallets. Generally, it is preferable to use local stone because it is more in character with the local landscape. It is usually cheaper, too.

Working with Stone

Building dry stone walls and rock gardens is like assembling a puzzle—you have to search for the stones that fit together.

By the time you have finished, you will have looked at every stone many times. However, sometimes even the most promising stone won't fit and will need to be altered. The idea is not to shape every piece but rather to make a few changes, such as knocking off a corner here and a bump there. Cutting and breaking stone is not difficult with the right tools, a basic understanding of how to hit the stone and a bit of luck. Tools you will need are: a heavy, chisel-edged mason's hammer (with a chisel on the head, 20- to 24-ounce size), a separate cold chisel and a few short pieces of wood (2 × 4s). Another, heavier blacksmith hammer (3- to 4-pound head) will also be helpful.

Before you begin, keep these rules in mind: Wear protection over your eyes. Whenever you hit a stone be sure it is resting on a softer surface, such as a piece of wood, to absorb the shock; if not, the blows may reverberate back up through the stone and break it in the wrong place. The wood itself may rest upon a hard surface such as

concrete, for stability, but you just cannot have one hard surface against another without a shock absorber between. Examine the strata or layers in the stone. It is easy to split stone along the strata, but very difficult to cut across them. Such dense stone as granite does not have strata, but still has faults and inconsistencies. It can be broken along these faults, if you hit them correctly. Often an unwanted corner can simply be knocked off by laying the stone on a piece of wood and hitting the corner with a downward stroke. Turn the stone so that the overhang of the corner is on top, and move the wood beneath out to the edge of the lower side of the stone for support, as shown below, left. This support can prevent the lower portion of the stone from splitting off.

When you need to be more precise and break along a line, first chisel a shallow groove along the desired breaking point, rest the stone on wood and chisel at an angle to avoid direct pressure. Next, rest the stone on the edge of a piece of-

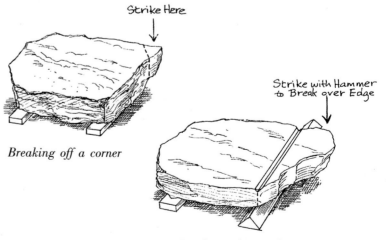

Strike Here

Breaking off a corner

Strike with Hammer to Break over Edge

Breaking along a line

wood and strike the extended unwanted portion with a downward stroke, as shown on page 32.

To cut a section from a thicker stone, use the same procedure, but strike the stone directly down on the groove. This will work best on stones without pronounced strata.

To remove a bump from the surface, place the chisel against the base of the bump at about a 45° angle and strike the chisel with the hammer a few times. This is easiest on stones with pronounced strata.

To split a stratified stone, place it on its side, on pieces of wood. Find a suitable fault, and place the chisel on the fault at a 90° angle. Strike the chisel several times and repeat, moving the chisel along the fault.

When using a chisel, technique and precision are very important. Always place it firmly on the spot you want to hit, then strike the chisel with the hammer. Any slippage of the chisel will reduce the force exerted on the stone.

Moving Stone

The weight of stone poses serious risks of hernias and injury to fingers, toes and backs for those who handle it improperly. Unfortunately, there are advantages of permanence and appearance to using the largest stones possible. With proper techniques, using rollers and prybars, large stones can be moved and incorporated into the rock garden.

Moderately sized stones, too large to lift and carry, can be rolled or flipped end to end along the ground. They can also be rolled into a wheelbarrow tipped on its side, or rolled up a plank onto a wagon. Select a wagon with the widest wheels possible to reduce the ruts made in soft ground. The same goes for wheelbarrows, with the further recommendation of an air-inflated tire, which makes the wheelbarrow much easier to use.

You can slide larger stones along the ground on a board. Use a prybar to pry or push them. The largest stones must be moved on rollers. You'll need three rollers in the form of pieces of iron or plastic pipe 3 to 4 inches in diameter and 2 to 3 feet long. Place plywood on top of the pipe and the stone on top of the plywood. As you push the stone along, move the back roller to the front.

Moving heavy stones can damage lawns, beds and even pavement. Damage to lawns and beds can be greatly reduced by waiting until the ground is frozen in winter. Protect pavement by covering it with sheets of plywood.

FORMULATING THE ROCK GARDEN DESIGN

Stone, in nature, is never disconnected; each block is always, as it were, a word in the sentence. Remember that urgently; boulder leads to boulder in an ordered sequence. A dump of disconnected rocks, with discordant forms and angles, is mere gibberish.
—Reginald Farrer,
The Rock Garden, 1912

It is one thing to observe natural rock formations and quite another to interpret this in the context of a rock garden in your backyard, especially the first time. It is also important to observe other rock gardens. This is where joining a group such as the American Rock Garden Society is a great help, especially for beginners. You can see how others have done it and learn from their mistakes and expertise.

Once you've decided on the location, the next question is, what will the rock garden look like? Before you even formulate your ideas, it is a good idea to spend some time observing natural rock outcrops and cliffs. Study the strata, cracks and fissures. Take your camera and photograph those that you find most interesting or instructive. You can also make drawings and sketches. If field observations aren't possible, go to the library and look over some geology books for good photographs.

Next, examine your own

This rock garden, on a level site, is built to resemble a rock outcrop. The tufa rocks are carefully placed to give the impression of being derived from one large rock.

stones. Roll them over, observe the different sides and imagine where they might be placed on the site, how they will look best once they are set in the ground. Study the site of your future garden. Make sketches, scratch out the locations of stones in the soil and even make cardboard templates or cutouts of various stones. Moving cardboard is much easier than moving stones, and you will be surprised by how much it helps you to visualize the design. Stakes and string may also help. Remember that when setting stone, the soil should come up to the widest part of the stone to give the impression that it widens further below the soil into the bedrock and con-nects with other surrounding stones. Some stones should be covered as much as two-thirds with soil, but the minimum is usually one-third, depending on shape. Deeply buried stones have greater stability.

The amount of stone you need will depend on the design and site of your rock garden. In a natural rock formation, more stone might be exposed on a steep site where the soil had washed off, while a gentle slope could be expected to retain more soil, with only a suggestion of the buried rock. A general rule is that stone should cover between one-sixth and two-thirds of the surface area of the rock garden. For practical reasons, you will need to have enough large stones conveniently spaced to double as stepping stones for access to all parts of the rock garden not accessible by a path. The stones should vary in size. Place the larger ones in the dominant positions, surrounded by smaller ones. Space them irregularly, but with a rhythm. Irregular spacing also allows planting areas of different sizes. Line up strata so that they run on the same angle in each stone to achieve a natural look. Tilt the strata and the stones back into the slope. Not only does this look more natural, but it also channels water back to plant roots.

GENERAL INSTRUCTIONS FOR BUILDING A ROCK GARDEN ON A SLOPE

1. Estimate the amount of stone. Unlike estimating stone for walls, there is no formula for figuring the amount of stone for building on a slope, because the amount of stone varies with the site, design and builder. A drawing or diagram with the estimated stone locations helps to estimate numbers and sizes. Then, go hand-pick your own stones at a quarry.

2. Examine the site to be sure grading channels the flow of water away from or around the rock garden, not over it.

3. The slope should be about 45° or less.

4. Remove the soil at least 18 inches deep, or plan for the rock garden to be 18 inches deep above the existing grade.

5. On the bottom, place a 4- to 6-inch layer of crushed stone, 2 inches or more in diameter. This provision for fast drainage is important in regions with high rainfall, unless there is a naturally gravelly or sandy subsoil. (On a steep slope or in dryer regions it can be eliminated.)

6. Next add a 2- to 3-inch-deep layer of ⅜- to ¾-inch stone chips.

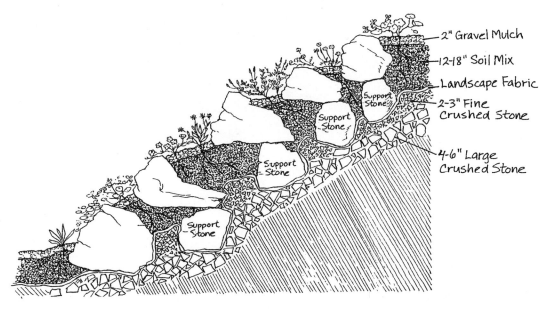

Cross-section of a rock garden on a slope

7. Place a layer of coarsely woven landscape fabric on top of the gravel to stop the soil from washing down into it. Or, use the traditional technique of a layer of leaves or coarse organic matter in place of the landscape fabric.

8. Place some large stones on the gravel layer to support the surface stones.

9. Working from the bottom of the slope, begin adding the surface stones, which should be large enough to be stable when walked on. Use your plan as a guide to position them.

10. Fill among and between the stones with soil mix, which should have a final minimum depth of at least 12 inches.

11. Allow everything to settle for a few months before planting, or make it settle by soaking thoroughly with water several times before planting.

12. Mulch with 2 inches of stone chips or gravel.

BUILDING A ROCK GARDEN OR RAISED BED ON A LEVEL SITE

1. Drainage is assured because it drains to all sides. If surrounded by walls, it is considered a raised bed. If positioned against a background, it will need a retaining wall along the back.

2. Be sure that all perennial grasses (including lawn grasses) and weeds are killed or completely eliminated from the site. Even root fragments produce plants that will become difficult to control among your rock plants.

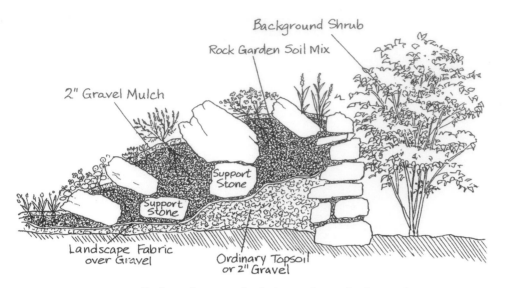

Rock garden on a level site against a background

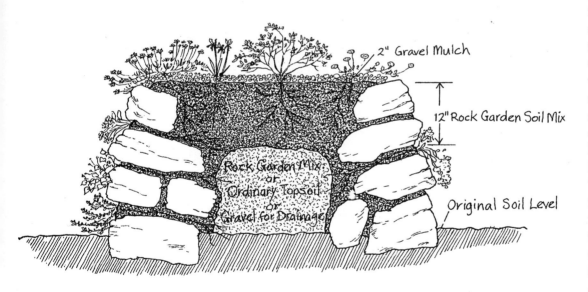

Cross-section of a raised bed

3. Make a mound to form the central core. Options:

a. Mound ordinary topsoil, which holds water in reserve for deep roots to tap into during dry periods.

b. Mound old tires, stacked and filled with rock garden soil mix.

c. Mound coarse 2-inch gravel in moist climates, and cover with a layer of landscape fabric to keep the soil mix from washing into the gravel.

4. Set support stones into the mound where the surface stones will be.

5. Roughly position surface stones on the mound. Place larger ones at the top to suggest the top of a rock outcrop, smaller stones down the slope and at the base.

6. Beginning at the bottom and working up, fill between the stones with the soil mix, which should be at least 12 inches deep. For a raised bed, fill behind the wall and plant as you build it.

7. Allow everything to settle for a few months before planting, or make it settle by soaking thoroughly with water several times before planting.

8. Mulch with 2 inches of stone chips or gravel.

LEDGE GARDENS

A rock garden running along a low slope can be fashioned into a simulated ledge or a low outcropping of exposed stone. It may take the place of a low retaining wall between different levels of lawn, for instance. A ledge is constructed in the same way as described for a rock garden on a higher slope. Setting the stone to look connected below ground is critical for success of the illusion. Take care to assure good drainage and that water does not flow over the rocks and planted area after a rain.

PATHS, PAVEMENT AND STEPS

Except for narrow raised beds and very small rock gardens, where everything can be easily seen and reached, you must build in a means of access. To a degree, this can be accomplished by arranging the stones among the plants so you can step from one to another, but as this can be awkward and clumsy, paths provide the best answer. Ideally, paths are a concentration of stones that coalesce into a trail through the rock garden. They are usually lower than the surrounding rock garden and may masquerade as dry stream beds. Paths need to look as natural as possible, and should be constructed of the same materials as the rest of the rock garden. Cut flagstone, brick or concrete paths are not in keeping with rock garden naturalism.

The most rudimentary type of path is a 3-inch layer of crushed stone on top of the soil. Sharp gravel packs better and forms a firmer surface for walking than rounded gravel. A thin layer of gravel, however, is not very durable and is liable to be poorly drained. Flat-surfaced rocks make a more stable path and are best set into a well-drained bed of gravel or sand to prevent frost heaving. The addition of a well-drained gravelly soil mix beneath the stones improves the path's suitability to plants that may intrude onto it. In shaded areas, organic surfacings of wood chips, bark or pine needles are more aesthetically appropriate, but they may harbor such pests as slugs and will need to be replaced more often because they rot away.

Safety and comfort are the primary considerations in constructing paths, and afford good reasons to build them correctly with proper drainage and firm footing. Rocks should be rough enough that they are not slippery when wet. Make paths at least 18 inches wide in a small garden, and at least 3 feet wide in large gardens, depending on traffic.

CONSTRUCTING A ROCK GARDEN PATH FOR PEOPLE AND PLANTS

1. Excavate the bed of the path 12 inches deep.
2. Fill 6 inches deep with sand or fine gravel.
3. Fill on top of the sand or gravel with gravelly rock garden soil mix (with extra crushed stone mixed in), leaving enough space for the depth of stones.
4. Set flat stones on the soil mix, level with each other.
5. Fill between stones with gravel mulch, 2 inches deep.

STEPS

Because rock gardens are not flat, you may want to integrate steps into the paths. Steps should be as wide as the paths, and comfortable to walk on. A single step should be no higher than 6 inches (the riser) and the level portion (the tread) should be between 14 and 19 inches deep. A higher riser with a shallower tread will encourage faster movement, while a lower riser and deeper tread will promote a more leisurely pace. As you build the steps, walk up and down to see how they feel.

Building rock garden steps

It is best to use a single long and thick stone for the riser, for stability. (Don't stand a thin stone vertically because it will push outward.) Use the same surfacing material as the rest of the path, such as flat stones or gravel, behind it. Set the steps in gravel to promote drainage and stability. Once set and contained, gravel is very stable and does not sink, settle or wash away as soil can. It also has the important added benefit of discouraging rodents that can dig and undermine the steps in time. In shaded woodsy gardens, you can substitute logs and pressure-treated wood risers for stone risers. Logs have a natural look, but regrettably, depending upon the kind of wood, do not tend to last a great many years. Pressure-treated wood, though durable, is rather artificial in appearance. It may be made to look more natural by rounding the corners.

STONE WALLS

Stone walls are unnatural landscape features constructed of natural materials. Though artificial, they take their inspiration from low cliffs. In the garden, they may take the form of a retaining wall against a bank or surround a raised bed. Dry stone walls contain no mortar, are the best for planting and are the easiest to build. A well-built dry wall will last for decades. They are low in maintenance, since there are few places for weeds to grow and wall plants tend to be long-lived.

The beauty of a dry wall is its flexibility and durability. If heaved by frost, it will generally settle back down when it thaws. As the stones are not bound together by cement, the wall cannot crack. If one of the stones is pushed out, you can pound it back in. (Make sure you cushion the stone by placing a piece of wood between the hammer and the stone.) Dry walls are also cheaper to build than walls with mortar, because they don't need the deep foundation required for a wet wall. There is some difference of opinion as to how deep the foundation of a dry wall needs to be and how it should be made. It does not need to go below the frost line, but in colder climates it should be deeper than in milder climates. I feel that in moderate climates (Zones 6 to 7), the base of the lower stones should be 3 or 4 inches below the soil level. This should be deep enough to hold them in place. In very cold climates, they should be a foot deep. Another way to make the foundation without burying the stones is to dig a trench, fill it with gravel and build the wall on top. Unfortunately, dry walls can't be built as high as wet walls. The safest maximum height per tier is about 3 feet, although it can be built higher if larger stones are used. For greater height, use multiple tiers, but do not attempt to go above 6 feet without the help and advice of an expert.

Vertical dry walls should be pitched back at an angle of about 10° into the slope. This amounts to 1 inch of pitch for 10 inches of height, or more simply, 1 to 2 inches per foot of height. To help get the angle right you can build an angle board by nailing together two boards with lengths equalling the height of the wall, angled 10° apart. Use a level to hold the vertical board in the vertical position and place the angle board against the wall. A less steep wall is called a stepped-back wall. It has a much gentler slope, perhaps an angle of 30° to 40° from vertical. The joints between the stone become more vertical and are easier to plant.

The strength and durability of a wall depends upon the skill with which you put it together. Fit the stones as closely and tightly as possible. Filling the spaces with smaller stone and using gravel behind the wall and in the soil are the best protection against rodents, which can become a severe problem otherwise. There are different opinions about what to use to fill behind a wall. Experts agree that ordinary topsoil should not be used. Most recommend a gravelly rock garden soil mix at least 6 inches deep behind the wall. Other gardeners recommend using gravel directly behind the wall for a couple of inches and the soil mix behind that. The theory behind this method is that the gravel provides excellent drainage, which

A well built, tight wall will last for decades and provide a home for many plants. Shown here is a wall at Stonecrop Garden, Cold Spring, NY.

prevents freezing water from heaving the wall. The plants like it because they can root through the well-drained gravel right back into the soil. When the soil has become dry and hard, water from rain or a sprinkler runs through the gravel behind the stones directly to the roots.

All the stone in a rock garden or rock wall should be of the same type, so make sure you obtain enough from the start to finish the job. Stone may vary in color or composition from one part of the same quarry to the next and you may not be able to match it if you need to obtain more later. You will never use every last stone, but the extras can be saved for repairs or alterations. The rule for estimating the amount of stone is that you will need about a ton of stone for every 30 square feet of wall face. A higher wall will need to be thicker, so it will require more stone. Use the largest stones you can handle, especially at the bottom. Most people can handle stones weighing about 100 to 150 pounds with a maximum of 250 pounds. Keep in mind that you can manage heavier stones if you take the time to move them properly and safely, but it will be more exhausting.

HOW TO BUILD A DRY WALL

1. Stretch a guideline (strong string or twine) along base of the wall and another along the top edge to keep it straight.
2. Excavate the foundation and into the slope a foot behind the wall.

3. Place the largest stones at the bottom for a secure foundation. Place the flat surfaces up, level with each other as a base for the rest of the wall. Fill between the stones with gravel to hold them securely.

4. Make the foundation wide enough to support the back of the wall so it will stand up even if the soil washes out.
5. Tilt the gravel and stones backward into the slope to allow water to drain to the

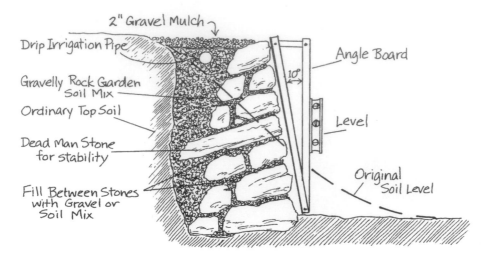

2" Gravel Mulch
Drip Irrigation Pipe
Gravelly Rock Garden Soil Mix
Ordinary Top Soil
Dead Man Stone for stability
Fill Between Stones with Gravel or Soil Mix
Angle Board
10°
Level
Original Soil Level

Dry stone retaining wall

plant roots. This will also increase the strength of the wall by shifting the center of gravity against the bank.

6. Build up the back of the wall as well as the front with stones, so that both ends of the stones are resting on other stones.

7. Whenever possible, face the roughest and most weathered surfaces out. It is an exercise in the art and craft of wall building to find planes and lines that relate to each other.

8. Most stones should point back into the wall. Small and narrow stones placed along the face of the wall will be pushed out by frost and the weight of surrounding stones. The wall will collapse with time around these weak points.

9. Periodically, lay a long "dead man" stone to project back from the front, into soil behind the wall for added stability.

10. Pitch or angle the wall into the slope as you build, 1 to 2 inches per foot of height, using your angle board for uniformity.

11. Set stones solidly and tightly so they can even stand without soil between, if soil washes out.

12. Fill spaces between stones and 6 inches deep behind the wall with gravelly soil mix, or use the gravel immediately behind the wall.

13. Set plants in the wall as it is built, spreading their roots. Small, pot-grown plants are best. Plan to cover just over half of the wall with plants when mature.

14. As you near the top, you can use smaller stones with less depth as there is less pressure pushing them out. They will also be easier to fix if they do shift out of place.

15. Bury a drip irrigation line about 4 inches deep behind the wall (optional).

Making A Hypertufa Trough
(Adapted from the American Rock Garden Society)

MAKING THE FORM (MOLD)

1. Use fine-grained Styrofoam insulation board, 1½ to 2 inches thick, which can be easily cut with a knife.
2. Hold the pieces together with 4-inch nails, three or four at each corner.
3. Reinforce with duct tape around the outside.
4. Make 3-inch-wide drainage hole(s) with rings of aluminum flashing, or with 1-inch-thick rings of PVC pipe.

HYPERTUFA RECIPE:

* 4–6 parts portland cement
  5 parts screened peat moss
  4 parts perlite
* A handful of copolymer fibers per trough
* Add cement pigment, gradually to preference
* 1 part liquid acrylic bonding agent
  Water, to moisten to putty-like consistency
* Available from concrete supply companies. These are the correct terms to use when buying these products.

PROCEDURE

1. Safety: Wear heavy rubber gloves to protect skin from the

caustic mixture, and a dust mask when working with dry ingredients.

2. Screen peat moss through ½-inch wire mesh to separate all the fibers and remove debris.

3. Separate and fluff copolymer fibers.

4. Measure and mix dry ingredients, except copolymer fibers.

5. Ingredients must be thoroughly mixed, so large quantities should be mixed with a cement mixer.

6. Add liquid acrylic bonding agent, and a little water to moisten slightly.

7. Add copolymer fibers.

8. Slowly add additional water. Add only enough water to make a dry putty consistency; too much will weaken the final product.

9. Mold and pound the mixture into the Styrofoam form at least 1 inch thick to shape the bottom and sides.

10. Completely wrap in plastic to prevent drying during the curing process. The mix will begin to harden in one hour and will be strong enough to take out of the mold in 24 to 48 hours (larger troughs cure faster because they generate more heat, which speeds the process). Troughs are still fragile when they're ready to uncover for finishing the surface, so use caution.

11. Disassemble the mold to finish the surface. Using a wire brush, scrape and distress the surface, rounding the corners and rough edges, to create the effect of weathered stone. Don't delay, or else the surface will become too hard to finish properly.

12. Finish the curing process in a shaded, frostfree, moist location for a month; rewet if surface seems dry, as water is important in the curing process.

13. Burn off protruding fibers with a propane torch, after surface is cured and dry (to avoid pit marks).

14. The finished trough will be ready to plant in three months and fully hardened in six months.

Troughs can also be created in a variety of other shapes. You can form them over inverted oval pans (such as turkey roasters), large bowls, or pressed coco fiber hanging basket liners (available at garden centers). Cover the form with a sheet of plastic to prevent the hypertufa from sticking. You can also make a free-form trough over a mound of hard packed sand. However it can be difficult to get a pleasing shape when working upside down.

Wearing rubber gloves, mold and pound the hypertufa mixture into the form, making walls at least one inch thick.

PLANTING AND GROWING GUIDE

TAILORING THE ROCK GARDEN CLIMATE

Few rock gardens are made in regions with ideal climatic conditions. You can overcome these climatic shortcomings with an understanding of plant needs, and how to modify the immediate microclimates in which they grow. The concepts are simple, and you can easily implement them in your rock garden design. Three basic needs of rock plants are:

1. They must not be crowded by larger plants.
2. They must have good drainage.
3. They must have good air circulation.

The Relationship Between
Light and Temperature

Most alpine plants have adapted to high light levels and cool temperatures. Saxatile plants from lower elevations may not be as fussy as alpines, but they generally prefer similar conditions. Light and temperature are closely related and they are the greatest challenges these plants face in lower elevations. Under ideal circumstances, most rock garden plants need full sun to nearly full sun, but the heat of direct sun in hot climates can be too much. Ideal summer temperatures are cool with normal high temperatures in the 70s and 80s° F, (rarely in the 90s), with cool nights. Such temperatures are found at higher elevations, and at lower elevations in New England, the Pacific Northwest and some coastal regions. In hotter climates rock garden plants are stressed and many may require shade from the midday heat to survive the summer. Morning sun is preferable to afternoon sun because it is cooler. In southern regions, where the heat of summer is intense for a long period, filtered shade (with spots of sun) may be necessary for most of the day.

This natural rock outcropping has been attractively planted to become a rock garden.

Aspect and Temperature

The direction that a rock garden faces is closely related to the amount of light and heat it receives. A slope facing south will be the hottest, while a slope facing north will be the coolest. If the north slope is not otherwise shaded it is an ideal place to grow many rock plants because it gets plenty of bright light without the associated heat of direct sun. In winter, it will also be markedly colder, but most alpines are very hardy and prefer to stay frozen. During the winter, the repeated freezing and thawing of a southern slope can heave the roots of small plants out of the soil if they are not protected.

In hot climates, many rock gardeners prefer an east-facing slope for the cool morning sun, which also has the advantage of drying off the morning dew quickly, and thus reducing disease problems. The great advantage of a rock garden built around a mound is the diversity of exposure you have to work with.

Rocks and Plants

The relationship of rocks and plants is complex. Many rock plants delight in having their roots tucked beneath a good stone where the soil is cool and moist. Rocks also create cool or warm microclimates on different sides. Shade lovers, or heat-sensitive individuals, may survive in a sunny garden if nestled on the north or east side of a stone, while those requiring a good summer baking or a warm pocket in winter can be induced to thrive on the southern side. Rocks absorb heat and moisture, which is released when needed. A warm stone acts as a radiator on a cold night and as a reservoir in a drought. These benefits are compounded when rocks are clustered together for greater mass. Clustered rocks also create the well-drained crevices in which so many rock plants thrive.

Air Circulation and Humidity

High-elevation rock plants are accustomed to plenty of air circulation. In nature, while these plants may be bathed in frequent fogs, they dry off quickly, keeping diseases at bay. At lower elevations, trees, hills and buildings all reduce air movement, which can pose problems for alpines and other rock plants. High humidity in many regions, particularly eastern North America, further complicates matters. Consequently, rock gardens should not be located in cramped quarters; instead they should always be in the most open site to maximize air circulation. Bear in mind that good air movement has the same result as lower humidity because it speeds drying of foliage, soil and rock surfaces.

Moisture, Drainage and Gravel Mulch

Many of the difficulties of cultivating rock garden plants are solved by the use of a gravel mulch. The stone does not retain surface moisture, as do organic mulches and the soil surface. Therefore it dries rapidly, so the plants can rest on a dry bed. Gravel warms more rapidly than an organic mulch or the soil surface, which helps to disperse moisture from around the plant. It also provides the perfect drainage around the stem of the plant at ground level. This stem at ground level, known as the crown of the plant, is its Achilles' heel. Most rock garden plants are lost when the crown rots. Gravel mulch, an inch or two deep, will reduce the risk of crown rot considerably.

This matter of drainage and dissipation of moisture cannot be overstressed. Anything that holds water around the plant is a threat to its well-being. I lost a wallflower (*Erysimum kotschyanum*) because a colony of ants had deposited a mound of clay subsoil under the foliage around the base of the stems. By the time I noticed, it was too late and it had rotted.

In nature, many mountain

and rock plants grow in well-drained soils composed of stone chips from weathered rock or glacial deposits, mixed with small amounts of organic matter. Meager amounts of organic matter result in soils low in nutrients, and also lower in rot-causing pathogens. In fact, many rock plants, adapted to such sterile soils, would be killed by the rich soils found naturally in valleys. Abundant nutrients also weaken them by stimulating overdrive growth. Such fast, soft growth is prey to numerous diseases. Stoney mountain soils provide excellent drainage all year, but allow roots to penetrate deeply in search of moisture and nutrients. Some stone also absorbs water that is released during dry spells. Almost without exception, drainage and aeration of these rocky soils are the secrets of success to growing rock plants.

The Summer Mugs

The combination of midsummer heat and humidity, described with dread by rock gardeners as "the mugs," is the downfall of many rock plants. As if the heat weren't bad enough, the high humidity inhibits a plant's ability to cool itself through evaporation, or even to dry off. This situation causes stress, which increases susceptibility to pests and diseases at a time when these foes are most active. One rock gardener I know recommends putting a fan on delicate plants during the mugs. Plants with tight, bun-like habits or woolly foliage are especially susceptible. (Foliage that is gray from a waxy or glaucous coating is more resistant to the mugs than woolly foliage.) Rock gardeners have discovered that encouraging good air circulation, soil drainage and rapid drying of foliage are the secrets to battling the mugs and adapting alpines and saxatile plants to their gardens.

Cold Frames and Alpine Houses—More Climatic Control

Cold frames and alpine houses protect tender plants against severe cold or unpredictable late spring or early fall frosts. A cold frame is a low structure covered with plastic or glass that admits light but excludes unwanted rain or cold. An alpine house is simply a greenhouse given over to growing alpines and other rock garden plants. Some rare plants from different climates require a dry period when it is usually raining in our gardens. Mediterranean bulbs, such as tulips, will benefit from staying dry (under cover) during the summer. During the winter, other kinds of plants may suffer or perish from dampness or dehydration from wind and sun, but otherwise be cold hardy. These problems are avoided in the wild because plants are protected by a cover of snow. In cultivation, an alpine house is an alternative solution. *Primula allionii*, from the snowy mountains of southern Europe, would surely perish outdoors in our winter rains. In an alpine house, however, where water can be controlled, this plant flowers much of the winter and early spring. The delicate, pale yellow, funnel-shaped *Narcissus romieuxii* from Morocco also flowers in late winter. Even in southern regions, where it is hardy, its flowers risk damage outdoors. However, it blooms to perfection in a cold frame or alpine house. An elaborate rock garden setup might include several cold frames and an alpine house. You can bring potted plants into the alpine house from the cold frames when they are in bloom so the plants can be admired more closely.

Cold frames may rest on top of the ground or be sunk into it, to take advantage of the insulation and warmth that rises out of the earth. Even without supplementary heat, a cold frame set into the ground may be 10° to 20° warmer than the outside air at night. Even a closed shallow frame resting on top of the soil is capable of

In the Alpine House at Wisley Garden, England, clay pots are sunk in sand to help control soil moisture and temperature.

This coldframe protects many small plants from harsh weather conditions, yet is easy to operate.

warding off a considerable night frost. Simple and inexpensive cold frames are available from garden suppliers. They can be made warmer by adding a horticultural heating cable, but this is seldom necessary. During warm weather, the cover is opened for ventilation, or removed altogether to prevent overheating. (Keep the cold frame covered with a wire mesh or screen if animals are a problem.) The bottom of a cold frame may have a layer of gravel, but more commonly it is filled with 4 to 6 inches of sand or fine grit. You can sink small pots of alpines in the sand up to their rims to support them, keep them moist, moderate soil temperature and minimize freezing and thawing.

Many alpine houses are not heated at all. Others are only heated enough to keep out frost, which protects water pipes and allows a greater range of plants to be grown. A minimum temperature of 35° to 40° F is adequate, so an alpine house is not expensive to operate. Whenever possible, keep the vents open to admit plenty of fresh air and to keep it as cool as possible when the sun shines. Use a fan at all times to circulate the air inside. While whole rock gardens can be constructed inside an alpine house, plants there are usually just grown in pots and sunk in sand beds.

The easiest plants grow well in the open rock garden when mature, but when young many need the protection of a cold frame or alpine house. More demanding plants prefer or require such protection throughout their lives. These structures provide a greater means of climate control. They also protect plants from such pests as rabbits and deer.

PLANTING ROCK PLANTS

After the rock garden is constructed and the soil has had time to settle as described in the previous chapter, it is ready to plant. Though potted plants can, in fact, be planted in the garden at any time, the best times to plant or transplant are early fall and early spring. These are the times when root growth is fastest. Early autumn is the best time of all for many plants, but don't plant later than a month before the first hard frost. If you must plant late, make sure you protect your plants against winter heaving with a mulch. Heaving can be a serious problem in climates where temperatures fluctuate radically. Freezing and thawing can pop or heave the roots of small plants right out of the soil. A mulch, which insulates the soil against rapid temperature changes, helps to prevent heaving. Wait until spring if winter heaving is a serious problem in your area or if you are planting less hardy plants. Summer, the season of heat and drought, is a risky time to plant because plants with root systems that have not been established yet must be watched very carefully for signs of water stress.

HOW TO PLANT

1. Dig a hole wide and deep enough so you can spread out the roots.
2. Tip the pot upside down in your palm and tap the pot upward to remove the plant while keeping the soil ball intact.
3. Loosen the roots around the outside of the ball of soil.
4. Plant at the same depth as the plant grew in the pot.
5. Firm the soil gently.
6. Mulch immediately.
7. Water thoroughly, and check to make sure that the water has penetrated.

PLANTING IN A WALL AFTER IT HAS BEEN BUILT

1. Use small plants, such as one- to two-year-old seedlings or well-established plants from cuttings.
2. Remove the soil as deeply as possible with a narrow trowel.
3. You may lift stones with a crowbar, but this might compromise the stability of the wall.
4. Push the root ends of the plant as far back as possible.
5. Replace the soil.
6. Keep the plants watered until they are well-established.

AFTERCARE

1. Watering is critical until the roots have grown deeply, especially in well-drained soil mixes or crevices in which the surface layers dry out quickly.
2. Watering may be less critical in the cool, moderate weather of spring and fall.
3. Shade young, severely disturbed transplants from the sun for a week or so, especially during hot weather. Use burlap supported by sticks, and moisten burlap to keep it cool during very warm weather.
4. Keep mulched and watch for heaving during winter.

CARE OF ROCK GARDENS

Watering

Proper watering is important to the well-being of rock plants, so it is essential to understand the needs of your rock plants. A well-drained soil mix is not necessarily a dry soil. The wilted or flagging appearance of plants on a sunny day does not mean that the soil is dry; it may mean that the plants just can't replace the water they lose through evaporation in the sun. Wait until evening or the next morning to see if the plants are still wilted before you decide to water. You can also dig down in the soil to feel if it is dry.

Moisture on foliage and around the plants promotes disease and rot. For most rock plants, therefore, you should water thoroughly and deeply on an infrequent basis, only when the soil is dry. The best time to water is in the morning or on dry, windy days when the foliage will dry as quickly as possible. During very humid weather, it is better to let the plants wilt than to water them at a time when the foliage will stay wet. An alternative is to water directly on the soil around the plant with a watering can or an underground watering system. In fall, reduce watering and let the plants go dry for a few weeks before frost to slow their growth and harden them off.

Trimming

Rock gardens require very little pruning compared to other kinds of gardens, but some judicious trimming can keep certain plants looking their best and neatest. The perfect time to trim is right after blooming. Some alpines grow a little too vigorously and become rather shaggy under the soft living conditions of many gardens. In these cases, a light shearing will keep them compact and in good form. Other plants seed themselves a bit too prolifically and need to have their seed pods removed before they mature.

Feeding

The most important thing to remember about feeding rock gardens is not to feed too much. Overfeeding will cause the plants to stretch and lose their compactness, as well as increase their susceptibility to disease. Nevertheless, general cleanup removes nutrients that might otherwise go back into the soil (and thus the plants), so a light feeding is advisable in most cases. Do not feed plants native to very poor, dry, rocky or sandy soils, ericaceous plants (rhododendron relatives) and very dwarf, tightly mounded plants that will stretch from overfeeding.

Use a slow-release organic fertilizer. Organic fertilizer is slow release because the nutrients are released gradually by the activity of bacteria that active at the same times the plants are growing and need feeding. Organic fertilizers are preferable because they feed plants gradually as needed and they do not burn plants. Top dress your rock garden by adding a ½-inch layer of the following mix each spring:

1 part leaf mold
1 part gravel
4 cups dried manure per bushel of mix

Weeding

Weeding is a necessary task, but it need not be a chore. It is an opportunity to get down close to the rock garden to examine and admire your plants. Elaborate tools are not required; you should have a long tool (such as an asparagus knife), to go after deep-rooted weeds, and an old kitchen fork for working around small plants.

During the first year of your rock garden, any seedlings will be weeds, but in successive years, some will be desirable seedlings from your plants. Learn to recognize these, and pre-serve them for yourself or your friends. This is especially important for annuals, biennials and short-lived perennials that need to reseed to perpetuate themselves.

Undoubtedly, the most troublesome weeds are the ones with perennial roots that run and creep underground and into your plants. When these get into a mat-forming plant, they are almost impossible to get out. Rhizomatous turf grasses, such as Kentucky bluegrass, and oxalis are good examples. Weed to get out all the roots, don't just pull off the tops. The best strategy for prolific seeders and annuals is not to allow them to seed themselves—ever! Weed them out before they bloom. This is called population control.

SEASONAL CARE SCHEDULE

Spring

- clean up debris that blew in during winter and remove winter mulch when weather has settled
- fix eroded spots
- reset heaved plants
- divide and replant over-crowded or overmature plants to rejuvenate in early spring
- replace dead or damaged plants
- give the garden a light feeding

Summer

- water in times of drought
- deadhead after blooming, especially plants that seed prolifically
- shear plants that tend to get leggy after bloom
- trim plants that crowd others
- weed as needed

Fall

- do a general cleanup
- clean off tree leaves to prevent their smothering small plants
- deadhead unless seedheads are attractive through winter
- do a final cleanup of weeds

Winter

- mulch to prevent frost heaving
- cover plants with evergreen boughs, salt marsh hay or coarse pine needles to prevent sunburn and windburn
- watch for heaved plants and push them back in the ground
- plan garden for spring and order plants

TROUGH GARDENING

Planting a Trough

1. Choose plants with similar light and soil requirements. Use dwarf varieties that will not quickly outgrow the trough.
2. Locate the empty trough in its final location, while it is still light and easy to move. Elevate shallow troughs on stone blocks.
3. Place a screen over the drainage hole(s). (A layer of gravel or other drainage materials is not considered necessary. Recent research has shown that it does not improve drainage.)
4. Fill with a free-draining but moisture-retentive soil mix, suited to the types of plants to be grown.
5. Compose stones and soil to create landscape effects, if de-sired. Soil may be mounded above the sides of the trough.
6. Add plants and topdress with a sharp gravel mulch to hold the soil in place.

Care of Troughs

The care a trough requires depends on the kinds of plants growing in it. Select a location that meets the light and temperature requirements of the plants. Full sun is preferred by most rock plants in the ideal climate, but in hot regions light shade or afternoon shade is advisable for many varieties. Shade plants, of course, require a location with less light. This reduces both heat and the need for water. Troughs planted with such succulents as hen and chickens (*Sempervivum*) and sedums will require less water, and are comparatively tolerant of neglect. Water should be provided only when the soil becomes dry, although a well-drained soil should protect against the effects of overwatering or a prolonged rainy spell.

Feed troughs very sparingly, to avoid encouraging the plants to outgrow their limited space. Most plants will be healthier—able to maintain proper forms and produce harder, thriftier growth—if kept on a meager diet.

Troughs containing hardy plants should be overwintered outdoors whenever possible. In climates with mild winters (zones 8–9), troughs can be left in the same location all year,

Troughs can be placed in or adjacent to the rock garden, but they will need more care than rock plants planted in the ground. Saxifraga op-positifolia flowers in this trough at the Berry Botanic Garden in Portland, Oregon.

perhaps with a covering of evergreen branches during the coldest weather. Where winters are moderately severe (zones 6–7) the troughs should be set down on the ground in a protected location, under evergreen shrubs or in a protected corner against a building out of the sun, with a cover of evergreen branches. Mulch pulled up around the sides helps to keep the roots warmer. In colder climates (Zone 5 or colder), it is generally best to keep the trough in the protection of a cold frame or alpine house, but this depends on the hardiness of the plants growing in them.

OBTAINING ROCK PLANTS

The easiest and most convenient way to obtain plants for your rock garden and troughs is to purchase them from a nursery. Local nurseries and garden centers with very good selections of plants may carry a few suitable rock plant varieties, but not many. You really need to get them from a specialty nursery, and this usually means mail order. Reputable mail order nurseries supply good quality plants and stand behind their products. (See page 91 for a list of nurseries.) Rock plants are small by nature and travel well. But be prepared: these slow-growing plants _will_ be small, and size is not a reflection of quality.

Another easy way to get plants is from friends and at periodic plant sales of the local chapter of the American Rock Garden Society (see page 10). These plants are inexpensive, and the sales raise money for the society. Since the plants are contributed by members, the grower is often standing there to answer any questions you may have.

Some gardeners prefer the challenge and fun of propagating their own plants. You can get cuttings from friends, but seed is readily available from specialty seed companies and from the annual seed exchange of the American Rock Garden Society, as well as other societies in Europe. Members around the world collect and save seed for the exchanges. Many varieties cannot be obtained by any other means, except possibly from members who have grown them.

GROWING SEEDS

Seeds vary in size and germination requirements. Seeds of hardy plants often have a built-in mechanism to delay germination until the weather is suitable in spring. One common mechanism is the requirement of a period of moist cold to break the dormancy. In nature, this requirement is usually satisfied by seeds falling onto moist soil in fall and lying there through the winter. Another protective mechanism found in very small seeds is that they will not germinate unless they are exposed to light. The presence of light is a sign that they are on the surface and not trapped under a layer of soil they can't break through. Some seeds will even grow immediately after sowing. It is common for seeds to have a combination of dormancy factors; but if you follow the procedure outlined here, you won't need to know all of them to get the seeds to grow. I just sow seeds whenever I get them and wait for them to germinate when they are ready.

I find that 4-inch-square plastic pots, 3 inches deep, are the most convenient size for starting seeds. The depth is important for proper drainage of the upper level of soil, and of course, the pots must have a drainage hole. Clay pots are porous and dry out faster, which is a real disadvantage in small pots. You can use a commercial potting soil or mix your own using:

1 part coarse sand or fine grit
1 part loam
1 part peat moss or leaf mold

Pasteurize this mix (as outlined on page 51) to eliminate pests, diseases and weed seeds. Diseases in particular can kill tender seedlings rapidly. Be sure to moisten and stir the potting soil before use, since dust-dry soil is very difficult to wet once it is in the pot.

Fill the pot with soil. Don't press it down, but tap the pot on a table to settle the soil, then smooth off the top. (The conventional wisdom has always been to put a layer of gravel in the bottom of the pot for drainage. Research has shown, however, that this is actually counterproductive and reduces drainage.) Sow your seed thinly over the surface of the soil. Very fine seeds can be mixed with a little dry sand to distribute them more evenly. Very large seeds can be pressed in just below the surface. Tweezers are often helpful.

The kind of seed will determine the material used to cover it. Dust-fine seed should only be covered with a very thin layer of sand. Larger seeds should be covered with about ¼ inch of gravel to hold the soil. The gravel is a perfect nurse material, because it holds the soil and seeds in place during watering and keeps the seeds moist. Gravel doesn't cake, so the seedlings can emerge easily. Once the seedlings have germinated, it provides a dry surface and helps to prevent damping off, a common seedling fungal malady. The gravel also prevents moss.

Be sure to label each pot with the name of the seed and the date it was sown. You might also want to make note of the number of seeds in the pot, and the seeds' source. Water the pots of seeds by setting them in a pan of water, then let them drain. Keep the soil moist, not wet, until the seeds germinate.

The pots cannot be kept outdoors, unprotected from animals and pelting rains, but they must be allowed to cool and warm with the seasons. They can even freeze. The moist cold treatment required by so many seeds before germination is called "stratification." As a general rule, the stratification requirement is satisfied by a temperature of around 40° F for six weeks to three months, but it varies from species to species. A cold frame or an alpine house is the perfect place to keep the pots. If you don't have such a place, you can keep them in a cold garage or enclosed porch, as I do. Another easy way to stratify seeds is to put the pots in a plastic bag and keep them in the refrigerator. Wherever you keep them, be sure that mice do not get into your seeds.

Seed germination of some species can be sporadic. Sometimes all the seeds of a certain type don't even germinate the same year. A good policy is to keep all pots of seed for at least two years before discarding them.

Immediately after germination, provide good light and air circulation—stagnant damp air promotes damping off. Begin feeding with a fertilizer that is high in phosphorous and low in nitrogen, diluted to half strength. The seedlings will be ready to prick-out (separate) and pot separately when they have two to five true leaves, or are 2 to 4 inches high. Put small plants in small pots, otherwise they won't be able to use up the excess water fast enough, and they will stay wet

Pasteurizing Soil

Research has shown that maintaining a balance of beneficial soil flora and fauna helps to suppress soil diseases. Pasteurization is not the same as sterilization because it kills only the harmful soil organisms, which die at a lower temperature. Bake the moist soil mix in a covered container (a roaster or casserole dish is good) in a 300° F oven or microwave, until it reaches 185° F. Measure the temperature with a candy or meat thermometer. Allow the soil to cool before use. Be prepared for a pungent cooked soil smell, which is unpleasant to some noses.

Saving and Storing Your Own Seed

Collect your own seed from the garden when it is ripe and the pod is open. Dry it thoroughly at room temperature. It can be sown immediately or stored in paper envelopes. Don't forget to label the envelopes. Keep the envelopes in an airtight container in the refrigerator with an envelope of silica gel or several grains of rice to absorb excess humidity. (Silica gel can be reactivated by heating it briefly in the microwave or a moderate oven to drive off the moisture.) Low moisture content of seeds is essential to prolonging storage life.

and rot. Apply a fine gravel mulch to each pot. Young plants in pots also need the protection of a cold frame if there is any danger of frost, or until they become large enough to withstand the elements, at which time they can be planted in the garden.

PROPAGATION

Cuttings

Many rock plants can be rooted from cuttings, some more easily than others. Each kind of plant roots best when the cuttings are taken at a particular time or stage of growth. Softwood cuttings are taken from half ripened wood in late spring to midsummer. Most will root in two to three weeks, and should be enclosed in a plastic bag to increase humidity and prevent wilting. Be sure to keep enclosed cuttings out of direct sun or they may overheat. Semi-hardwood cuttings are taken in midsummer when they are more mature. They are less subject to wilting, and small leafed plants may not need to be covered, just sprinkled with water daily. Hardwood cuttings are taken in early winter, when the plants are dormant. Because they are leafless, hardwood cuttings are often nearly covered with the rooting medium to keep them moist. They must be kept in a cold frame until spring, when they should begin growing.

Cuttings should be taken early in the morning or on a cloudy day, when they contain the most water. Put the cuttings in a plastic bag immediately to keep them from wilting. Wilting will greatly reduce their chance of success. Short cuttings of young wood, with several nodes, usually root best. The biggest problem with rock plants is getting cuttings large enough to handle.

Your choice of rooting medium depends on your preference and the kind of plant you want to root. The medium must be very open and well-aerated to stimulate roots and hold plenty of moisture. They must also be free of disease organisms, and so should not contain any soil or leaf mold. Sharp sand, vermiculite, perlite and coarse peat moss are all suitable either alone or in combination. Peat moss is acidic and should be included for acid-loving plants. Be sure to use a clean pot. You can sterilize pots by soaking them in a solution of 1 part chlorine bleach to 10 parts water.

Prepare the cuttings by removing the leaves from the lower part of the stem that will be inserted into the soil. Using a very sharp instrument, such as a razor blade, make a clean cut just below the lowest node. Some plants root better from heel cuttings, which are from a small side branch with a small piece of the main stem (the "heel") still attached. To take a heel cutting, tug downward to pull off a side branch. Dip the bottom tip of the cutting in rooting hormone powder and shake off the excess. Use a pencil or stick to make a hole in the rooting medium before inserting the cutting to avoid rubbing off the hormone powder. A horticultural heating cable under the pots will warm the medium, and stimulate the cuttings to root more rapidly and strongly. When the cuttings offer resistance to a gentle tug, they are rooted.

An alternative but less-known propagation technique is the use of root cuttings. Cut pieces of root an inch or two long from the parent plant, and insert them upright or on an angle in the rooting medium, with the tips showing. In time, they form new shoots at the top. The most important thing is to keep the up end up. When turned upside down, root cuttings may fail to grow. Root cuttings are best taken in late fall or early spring, and should be kept cool during the winter. Geraniums (*Geranium* spp.) and pasque flower (*Pulsatilla vulgaris*) both grow from root cuttings.

Division

The easiest method of propagation in the garden is division of the crown of the plant. The best time is early spring, while the plant is still dormant. Fall is a more risky time because without fully established roots, the divisions may be heaved out of the ground by frost. To divide a plant, dig it out of the ground, and cut or pull apart the center, detaching sections with both stems (or buds) and roots attached. Replant each piece at the same depth that it grew before, and spread the roots in the fresh soil. Water well and mulch. No further special care is usually necessary.

Layers

An easy way to propagate a difficult plant is to layer it, by bending a branch down to the soil and inducing it to take root while still attached to the parent plant. This is most commonly done with difficult woody plants, such as rhododendrons, but it is also a good method for mat-forming plants. Pin a stem down to the soil with a hairpin or stone. Cut or scrape the lower side of a woody stem to obstruct sap flow and then dust the cut with hormone powder. Cover with soil. Rooting may take several months. When rooted, cut the stem and allow the young plant to establish itself, before you transplant it on a cool, overcast day.

Aftercare of Young Plants

Once rooted, cuttings should be hardened off by gradually uncovering them, moving them into more light, and exposing them to wind and rain. Feed with a half-strength liquid fertilizer. When they have begun to make growth they can be potted separately. The same applies to seedlings. They should all be grown outdoors as soon as possible. A cold frame provides the ideal environment because it can be fully opened in good weather for maximum exposure, and closed when necessary. It also provides protection for small pots from animals and stray feet, even when open. If necessary, wire mesh can be placed over the top to exclude animals.

Labels For Your Plants

Knowing the identity of a plant is vital in providing the proper care, but keeping track of your plants and their names can be a bewildering task. Labeling is the easiest way to keep tabs on your plants. In addition to their names, labels serve to mark the location of small plants or those that are not visible when dormant. Each pot of seeds and cuttings should also be labeled.

Labels are available in many shapes and sizes, made of plastic, metal or wood. Of course, small labels are best for tiny rock plants. I've found that plastic labels are the most convenient for pots, where appearance is not especially critical. Out in the garden, plastic labels are unsightly. They also have a limited life unless they're buried to protect them from the ultraviolet rays of the sun, which break down the plastic and make it brittle. Zinc labels are more durable outdoors and have a less obtrusive color. Be sure they have long stems, to anchor them securely against frost heaving in winter. I've known labels to come out of the ground in winter and blow away.

I write on all labels with a number 2 pencil. It is more durable than indelible marker and has a finer point, which is particularly good for writing on small labels. If you find the pencil difficult to read, write over it with the indelible marker.

Record as much information on labels as you find useful and have space for. In addition to the technical name, the common name might be helpful if you are unfamiliar with technical names. When starting seeds or cuttings, record the date, the source and notes on methods. Labels help to take the mystery out of gardening.

PLANT PORTRAITS

PLANT PORTRAIT KEY

There is seemingly no end to the variety of plants that are adaptable to rock gardens. My selection of alpines and rock plants to highlight in the following pages is, necessarily, incomplete. Ease of growth was a primary criterion. A few of these plants require greater skill, but these amply reward the grower with their exquisite beauty.

I have broken up the different kinds of plants into separate sections of perennials, shrubs, bulbs and conifers. A perennial is a plant that is not woody, but will grow from the same root year after year. It may be evergreen or deciduous (lose leaves in the winter), depending upon the species. A shrub is a plant with several woody stems or trunks arising from the soil, that lives from year to year. They may be evergreen or deciduous. A subshrub is intermediate between a perennial and a shrub with nearly woody stems. A bulb is a plant that grows from an underground organ each year (i.e., a tulip). In this book, I am using "bulb" to include corms (i.e., crocus) and rhizomes (i.e., windflower). A conifer is a woody plant (many of which are trees) that reproduces by bearing cones, rather than flowers. Dwarf conifers are slow-growing variants or mutations, the smallest of which make good rock garden plants. Most are evergreen and have attractive foliage all year long. May this selection of plants serve as an enjoyable introduction to the world of rock gardening.

Scientific names of rock garden plants are in boldface italics. They are essential for precision when discussing specific plants. Common names vary so much from region to region that readers and nursery owners alike cannot always be sure what they are referring to. Scientific names can tell you something about the plants by showing their relationships to each other.

Scientific names are usually based on Latin or Greek, languages that don't change and so will always be understood internationally. Each name is a subdivision of the former. The first name is the genus which is always capitalized. The second name is the species, which is usually not capitalized. All plants have at least these two botanical names.

Additional names may follow to designate a variety, subspecies or a cultivar. Varieties and subspecies usually occur naturally, in the wild. They are written in the same way as the species name. *Cultivar* means *culti*vated *vari*ety—cultivars are created or found only in gardens. The name is usually a modern-language name, is not italicized, is always capitalized and is placed in single quotes (i.e., the St.-John's-wort cultivar 'Citrina').

Many garden plants are hybrids. This may be indicated in the name by an "×" (but it is not required). Thus we know that lemon thyme, *Thymus × citriodorus*, is a hybrid of other species. Cultivars are often hybrids such as *T. × citriodorus* 'Aureus' which has golden foliage.

Lewisia cotyledon, *one of the most prized alpines, is seen growing wild in a serpentine scree on Fiddler Mountain in the Siskiyou Mountains, OR.*

Sometimes there is more than one scientific name for the same plant. One name is considered to be more correct than the others. When other names are in common use, the synonyms are given in parentheses immediately following the preferred name.

Phonetic pronunciation of the scientific name is in parentheses.

Common name of the plant is in boldface type.

Hardiness: Zone refers to the USDA Plant Hardiness Map (pages 92–93). This map is based on average minimum winter temperatures, the most important factor determining hardiness, and the zone given is the estimated northern limit. Other factors affect plant survival and health, too. High summer temperatures in the Southeast may kill or limit a plant's growth, whereas the same plant will grow successfully in the cooler summers of an equivalent zone of winter cold along the Pacific coast. Soil drainage can improve a plant's ability to survive both winter and summer conditions. Air circulation is beneficial in summer when it keeps foliage dry, but harsh winds in winter may cause harmful dehydration at below freezing temperatures. A reliable winterlong snow cover enables low shrubs and perennials to survive under the snow much further north than would be possible without it, because it protects from severe temperatures, exposure, and dampness. Hardiness is an estimation, at best. When a range is given, it indicates that hardiness may vary slightly with individual varieties, or is borderline between two zones.

The average hours of sun needed per day is indicated by symbols.
○ Full sun: 6 or more hours of strong direct sunlight per day.
◐ Partial shade: 3 to 6 hours of direct sunlight, light dappled shade all day or high shade all day. (High shade means that the shade is cast by high branches, allowing plenty of diffuse, indirect light to come from the sides.)
◫ Deciduous shade: Shade cast by deciduous trees and shrubs in summer when in leaf. In late fall, winter and early spring any plants underneath receive full sun. This is of value to early spring bulbs that need winter sun for good growth, but are dormant during summer.
● Full shade: Little or no direct light, usually shaded by low branches with dense foliage to provide relatively dark conditions.

Size: Two measurements are given, separated by an "×." The first is the height. The second is the spread or width of the plant. These sizes are estimates of the typical size the plant is expected to reach in most gardens, but it can vary with soil fertility and climate. Since dwarf conifers never stop increasing in size, the size given is based on the 10-year estimate, to give a comparison of vigor between varieties. With low soil fertility or when restricted in a trough, growth will be slower.

Season of bloom: This is a rough guide to the time a plant will bloom, and will vary from North to South and with summer heat, which can speed or slow growth. SP = Spring, SU = Summer, F = Fall, E = Early, M = Middle, L = Late, i.e., ESP = Early Spring.

Native to: The region or country where a plant grows is given as a clue to cultivation and for general interest.

Uses: The best rock garden uses are given as a quick reference.

Characteristics: Describes appearance and suggests useful varieties and cultivars.

Related species: Describes other related species and hybrids useful in the rock garden.

Cultural information: Explains optimal soil, placement and care.

PERENNIALS

Achillea tomentosa (a-KILL-ee-yah toh-men-TOH-sa) **woolly yarrow,** ES ○ ◐
Zone: 3
Size: 6" × 12"
Native to: Europe, N. Asia
Uses: Rock garden, wall, trough
Characteristics: Spreading rhizomes form an attractive gray mat of low, ferny, woolly foliage. The flat heads of yellow flowers are held on somewhat lax 6-inch stems. 'Maynard's Gold' has golden yellow flowers.
Related species: The hybrid 'King Edward' has more subtle soft yellow flowers. *A. chrysocoma* is similar with more densely hairy foliage. *A. ageratifolia* (*serbica*) (Balkan mountains, Zone 5, 6"×12") has gray, lance-shaped leaves and white flowers.
Cultural information: Blooms best in a well-drained soil of poor to moderate fertility in full sun. The woolly foliage predisposes this yarrow to summer rots in confined spots with poor air circulation, but it tolerates some shade.

Aethionema grandiflorum (e-THEE-oh-nee-ma gran-dee-FLOR-um) **stone cress, Persian candytuft,** MSP ○
Zone: 6
Size: 6"–8" × 15"
Native to: Lebanon and Iran
Uses: Rock garden, wall, scree, trough
Characteristics: This is a pink version of the ever-popular candytuft (*Iberis*), to which it is related. Its beautiful deep blue-green foliage is attractive all year long.
Related species: 'Warley Rose'

(4"×12") is a smaller hybrid and perhaps the most popular type.
Cultural information: Prefers limey or neutral soils with good drainage and is drought tolerant. Shear lightly after flowering.

Allium senescens glaucum (AL-lee-um se-NE-senz GLAW-cum) **flowering onion,** LSU ○
Zone: 5
Size: 10" × 8"
Native to: China
Uses: Rock garden, alpine meadow, wall, trough
Characteristics: Unlike many bulbous onions, these onions grow throughout the summer. The clumps of narrow, slightly twisted grayish leaves form a tight groundcover from which rise lavender-pink flowers. The foliage has an oniony scent when bruised.
Related Species: *A. thunbergii* (Japan, Zone 4, 12"×8") has narrower leaves and deeper rose-pink flowers in autumn.
Cultural information: An ordinary soil with reasonable drainage will suit these onions.

Alpine aster; see ***Aster***

Alpine poppy; see ***Papaver***

Androsace sarmentosa (an-DRA-say-see SAR-men-toh-sa) **rock jasmine,** LSP-ESU ○ ◐
Zone: 5
Size: 2"–8" × 18"
Native to: Himalayas and W. China
Uses: Rock garden, wall, scree, trough
Characteristics: The evergreen

Achillea *'King Edward'* (*See* A. tomentosa)

Aethionema *'Warley Rose'* (*See* A. grandiflorum)

Allium senescens

Androsace sarmentosa

A. *sarmentosa* is the most popular species of this highly regarded group of alpines. In winter the rosettes are composed of small, tight leaves covered with silvery hairs. The summer leaves are larger and fewer in number. The rosettes spread by runners into an open mat and bear clusters of small pink flowers.

Cultural Information: The rock jasmines prefer a well-drained, gritty soil in full sun, though I have grown this one in partial shade quite successfully.

Antennaria dioica (an-TEN-air-ee-a dy-OH-y-ka) **pussytoes,** SP ○ ◑

Zone: 3
Size: 4" × 18"
Native to: northern regions of Asia, Europe, North America
Uses: Rock garden, alpine meadow, wall, scree, trough
Characteristics: This low, creeping evergreen groundcover with fuzzy gray foliage roots readily. Clusters of pink flowers are held above the low foliage. A. *dioica rosea* is the most common variety, with pink flowers. 'Nyewood Variety' (3"×12") is

shorter, with smaller, more compact leaves and deep carmine pink flowers. It is especially good for troughs.
Cultural information: Grows best in poor, dry soils in a hot location, but it should not be allowed to dry out severely.

Aquilegia flabellata (a-KWIL-ee-jee-a fla-BEL-lay-ta) **col-umbine,** MSP-LSP ○ ◑

Zone: 3
Size: 4"–18" × 4"–12"
Native to: Japan
Uses: Rock garden, alpine meadow, wall, scree, trough
Characteristics: The tall, deciduous, long spurred columbine hybrids are familiar woodland and flower garden plants. Many dwarf kinds are equally suitable for rock gardens. A. *flabellata* is now commonly available, usually in its dwarf forms, which are the only ones really suitable for rock gardens. They are compact plants with one or two flowers per stem, held above blue-green foliage. 'Nana Alba' (4"–6" × 6") has white flowers. A. *f. pumila* is the same size with bicolored purple-blue and white flowers.

Related species: Many other more diminutive species are equally easy to grow in the rock garden. A. *bertolonii* (S. Europe, Zone 3, 3"–4" × 4") is a choice little alpine with large, deep blue flowers. A. *discolor* (Spain, Zone 8, 4"–6" × 6") has blue flowers with white centers.
Cultural information: The alpine columbines prefer sun to light shade in a well-drained soil, especially with a gravel mulch to prevent crown rot. All sow themselves freely.

Arabis blepharophylla (AH-rah-bys blef-ar-oh-FY-la) **rock cress,** LSP ○ ◑

Zone: 3
Size: 6" × 12"
Native to: North America
Uses: Rock garden, alpine meadow, wall, scree, trough
Characteristics: This evergreen features a basal tuft of hairy leaves, from which rises a stem bearing numerous pink flowers. 'Spring Charm' has more deeply colored pinkish purple flowers.
Related species: The more common A. *caucasica* (S. Europe, Zone 4, 12" × 8") is closely

Antennaria dioica

Aquilegia flabellata 'Nana Alba'

Arabis caucasica *'Flore Plena' (see* A. blepharophylla*)*

Arabis sturii

related or synonymous with *A. alpina*. It forms a loose mat of low, sprawling stems with hairy leaves and produces white flowers in early to late spring. 'Flore Plena' bears double flowers for the remarkable period of six weeks.
Cultural information: Easy to grow in any lean soil with good drainage.

Arabis sturii (AH-rah-bys stir-ee-eye) **rock cress,** MSP ○ ◑
Zone: 4
Size: 6" × 12"
Native to: unknown
Uses: Rock garden, wall, scree, trough
Characteristics: The origin of this tough little evergreen is shrouded in mystery, but it is believed to be a dwarf form of the closely related *A. procurrens*. I prefer *A. sturii* for its tight low mat of little, shiny, leathery green leaves. The clusters of small white flowers are held above on wiry stems.
Related species: A. procurrens (S.E. Europe, Zone 5, 12"×18") is less compact and more spreading in habit. It likes to climb through the spaces in a stone wall, but is less drought tolerant than *A. sturii. A. androsacea* (Turkey, Zone 4, 2"×6") is a more discriminating alpine, which grows best in screes and troughs.
Cultural information: Easy to grow in any lean soil with good drainage.

Arenaria montana (ah-ren-AIR-ee-a mon-TAN-a) **sandwort,** ESU ○
Zone: 5
Size: 8" × 24"
Native to: S.W. Europe
Uses: Rock garden, wall, scree, trough
Characteristics: This old-time, evergreen favorite is related to pinks (*Dianthus*) and bears similar large white flowers in profusion. This long-lived plant forms a mat of dark green foliage, emanating from a central crown, that will cascade spectacularly from the cracks in a stone wall. Unlike many plants, the stems do not root readily into the ground.
Related species: A. verna (Minuartia verna) (Europe, Zone 2,

Arenaria verna *(see* A. montana*)*

1"×12") is a low, rounded, mat-forming plant with tiny starlike white flowers. It is ideal for planting among the stones in a path, or in troughs.
Cultural information: Almost any well-drained soil will suit these sandworts. Seed is the only reliable means of propagating *A. montana*.

Armeria maritima 'Dusseldorf' (see A. caespitosa)

Aster alpinus

Aubretia deltoidea

Armeria caespitosa (ar-MER-ee-a ses-spee-TOH-sa) **thrift, sea pink,** SP ○

Zone: 3

Size: 3" × 6"

Native to: Spain

Uses: Rock garden, alpine lawn, wall, scree, trough

Characteristics: (Syn. *A. juniperifolia*) The smaller size of this evergreen thrift makes it one of the best for use in rock gardens and troughs. Spherical pink flower clusters are held above tufts of narrow foliage for an effective contrast to mat and bun-shaped rock plants. 'Bevan's Variety' (5"×6") is somewhat larger with more deeply colored rose flowers.

Related species: A. maritima (Europe, Asia Minor, N. Africa, North America, Zone 3) is a more commonly grown species. While variable in height, it is seldom over 12 inches.

Cultural information: Thrift is easy to grow in a neutral or limey soil with reasonable drainage.

Aster alpinus (AS-ter al-PY-nus) **alpine aster,** SU ○ ◑

Zone: 2

Size: 8"–10" × 12"

Native to: European Alps

Uses: Rock garden, alpine meadow, wall, scree, trough

Characteristics: Blue or white daisy flowers with yellow centers above low tufts of foliage for much of the summer make this deciduous perennial a valuable addition to the rock garden.

Cultural information: An easy-to-grow plant that is not particular about soil as long as it is well drained.

Aubrieta deltoidea (aw-BREE-sha del-TOY-dee-a) **purple rock cress,** SP ○ ◑

Zone: 4

Size: 6" × 18"

Native to: Sicily, Greece, Turkey

Uses: Rock garden, wall, scree, trough

Characteristics: The evergreen purple rock cress has been a favorite in rock gardens and walls for years. It is widely available as seed and plants in many varieties. It forms a low mat, which is covered with purple, reddish-purple or white flowers in spring.

Cultural information: Prefers, but does not require, a limey soil. Drainage, however, is essential and aubretias do better in walls and crevices. They resent heat and should not be exposed to the full force of afternoon sun in summer. Shear lightly after bloom.

Aurinia saxatilis (or-IN-ee-a saks-ah-TIL-is) **basket-of-gold,** ESP-MSP ○ ◑

Zone: 4

Size: 8"–16" × 16"

Native to: S. and C. Europe, Turkey

Uses: Rock garden, wall, scree, trough

Characteristics: (Syn. *Alyssum saxatile*) This is a sprawling, evergreen perennial with almost woody stems and long narrow leaves. Flowers are golden yellow. 'Citrina' has soft lemon-yellow flowers. 'Sunny-border Apricot' bears soft apricot-yellow flowers. Most varieties are too large for small rock gardens, but 'Tom Thumb' (3"×10") is smaller and suitable even for troughs.

Cultural information: These drought-tolerant plants are adaptable to ordinary (well-drained) soils. Shear or trim after flowering for compactness.

Aurinia saxatilis (*shown with purple* Aubretia deltoidea)

Campanula carpatica
(see C. portenschlagiana)

Basket-of-gold; see *Aurinia*

Bearded iris, dwarf; see *Iris pumila*

Beard-tongue; see *Penstemon*

Bell flower; see *Campanula*

Campanula portenschlagiana (kam-PAN-ew-la poor-TEN-shlog-ee-ay-na) **bell flower,** LSP-ESU ○ ◑
Zone: 3
Size: 6" × 18"
Native to: Dalmatia
Uses: Rock garden, wall, scree, trough
Characteristics: Campanulas are valued most highly for their blue flowers, though some are white. Many are too large for the rock garden, but plenty of small species remain from which to choose. *C. portenschlagiana* (*C. muralis*) is one of the easiest of the small species with deep blue flowers and a clumping habit. The

closely related *C. poscharskyana* will colonize a wall effectively, but it spreads too vigorously in the garden.
Related species: C. carpatica (Carpathian Mountains, Zone 4, 6"–12"×18"–24") is useful for its mid to late summer blue or white flowers, but except for the dwarf forms, is too vigorous for small rock gardens—it sows itself into smaller neighbors too freely. *C. carpatica turbinata* (4"–8"×12") is a dwarfer variety with hairy leaves. *C. cochleariifolia* (*C. pusilla*) (European mountains, Zone 4, 2"–6"×12") is a diminutive plant with roving rhizomes that are excellent for wandering through a stone wall. *C. elantines fenestrellata* (Italy and Yugoslavia, Zone 4, 6"×18") is a compact species suited to walls and troughs.
Cultural information: Bell flowers are easy to grow in well-drained, gritty soils. *C. portenschlagiana* and *C. carpatica* are adaptable to ordinary soil and the easiest to grow. Slugs can be troublesome with some species. Deadheading will prolong the bloom of many species.

Campion; see *Silene*

Candytuft; see *Iberis*

Candytuft, Persian; see *Aethionema*

Carex conica 'Variegata' (KAH-reks KON-ee-ka) **sedge,** ◑
Zone: 5
Size: 6" × 10"
Native to: Japan
Uses: Rock garden, alpine meadow, trough

Carex morrowii *'Variegata' (see C. conica)*

Characteristics: These evergreen clumps of narrow, grasslike leaves edged with white are an excellent contrast for dark green conifers and rhododendrons.
Related species: C. morrowii 'Variegata' (Japan, Zone 6, 12"×18"), also striped with white, is more commonly available, but is larger growing.
Cultural information: Prefers a shaded location in a rich, moist soil, but will tolerate more sun in cool climates.

Catch-fly; see *Silene*

Cheddar pink; see *Dianthus*

Cinquefoil, golden; see *Potentilla*

Columbine; see *Aquilegia*

Corydalis lutea (KOR-y-dal-lys LEW-tee-a) **corydalis,** SP-F ◑
Zone: 5
Size: 16" × 16"
Native to: Europe

Corydalis lutea

Dianthus
gratianopolitanus

Erigeron compositus

Uses: Wall
Characteristics: The delicate appearance of these ferny plants with flowers like those of bleeding hearts, is deceiving, because they can over-power smaller plants with their vigorous nature. Nevertheless, these deciduous perennials are lovely colonizers of walls, since they seed freely. *C. lutea* has blue-green foliage and yellow flowers.
Related species: C. ochroleuca (S. Europe) is much the same as *C. lutea,* except that the flowers are cream colored. *C. cheil-anthifolia* (W. China, 12"×18") is more ferny in appearance with bright green leaves and spikes of golden yellow flowers.
Cultural information: These cory-dalis prefer, but do not require, a neutral to limey soil. They have deep roots for drought tol-erance. The above species are the easiest to grow and seed too freely to be allowed near your small rock plants.

Creeping gypsophila; see *Gypsophila*

Cress, purple rock; see *Aubrieta*

Cress, rock; see *Arabis*

Cress, stone; see *Aethionema*

Daisy, globe; see *Globularia*

Dianthus gratianopolitanus (dy-AN-thus gra-TAN-oh-pol-ee-tan-us) **Cheddar pink,** LSP-ESU ○ ◐
Zone: 3
Size: 4"–6" × 12"–18"

Native to: W. and C. Europe
Uses: Rock garden, alpine meadow, wall, scree, trough
Characteristics: The evergreen dwarf pinks are the quintessen-tial rock garden plants. Of the many species and hybrids, *D. gra-tianopolitanus* (*D. caesius*) is perhaps the most easily ob-tained and grown. It forms a tight low mat or mound of fine glaucous foliage, with a profu-sion of fragrant, deep rose-pink flowers held above on straight stems. 'Tiny Rubies', possibly a hybrid, has rosy red blooms.
Related species: D. × allwoodii (8"×12") is a group of hybrids in a range of colors from white to salmon and rose pink, some of which are bicolors. Although rather large for the rock garden and short-lived, they are valued for their long bloom season. *D. arenarius* (N. Europe, Zone 5, 6"×12") forms a low mat of green foliage with very fragrant, deeply fringed white flowers. It is more shade tolerant than most pinks. *D. pavonius* (*D. ne-glectus*) (S.W. European Alps, Zone 5, 4"×4"), glacier pink, is not for the beginning rock gar-dener due to its tiny size and slow habit of growth. It is, how-ever, the epitome of an alpine with low tufts of stiff, pointed leaves and large pink flowers. When provided with a gritty soil it will be long-lived and is ideally suited to a scree or trough. It is one of the pinks that does not prefer lime. *D. simulans* (moun-tains along the Greek-Bulgar-ian border, Zone 4, 3"×5") is another diminutive alpine for screes and troughs. Rose-red flowers above spiny tufted gray foliage. *D. superbus longicalyci-nus* (Korea, Zone 4, 12"–

16"×20") has an oversized, leggy habit suitable for only the largest rock gardens, but it is highly desirable for its late summer and early fall bloom. The lavender-pink flowers are composed of deeply cut, fringed petals. Deadhead to prolong bloom. Comes true from self-sown seeds.
Cultural information: Most of the pinks are lime lovers, though they can survive with-out it if the soil is not too acid. The tight habit of these dwarf pinks predisposes them to sum-mer rots if not planted in an open location with good drain-age. Working soil between the foliage (down around the stems) in spring helps to avert this and it encourages new roots to form. Otherwise they are easy to grow. Self-sown seedlings generally do not come true but are nevertheless attractive.

Dwarf bearded iris; see *Iris pumila*

Dwarf flower-of-Jove; see *Lychnis*

Erigeron compositus (ER-y-jer-on com-POS-y-tus) **erigeron,** SP-ESU ○
Zone: 5
Size: 10" × 10"
Native to: N. America
Uses: Rock garden, scree, trough
Characteristics: This woolly, gray-foliaged plant bears pale blue to white daisies with yel-low centers. It forms a long tap-root and seeds in the garden.
Cultural information: These plants are easy to grow pro-vided they are given a well-drained, gritty soil in a hot, dry location.

Flowering onion; see *Allium senescens glaucum*

Flower-of-Jove, dwarf; see *Lychnis*

Gentian; see *Gentiana*

Gentiana septemfida

(JEN-shee-an-a sep-tem-FID-a) **gentian,** LSU ◐
Zone: 3
Size: 18" × 18"
Native to: Mountains of W. and C. Asia
Uses: Rock garden, alpine meadow
Characteristics: Above all, gentians are valued for their true blue flowers and are another of the quintessential rock garden plants. *G. septemfida* is also highly valued for its late summer clusters of flowers at the ends of arching stems. It is one of the easiest to grow. Although rather large, they can be underplanted with spring flowering bulbs.
Related species: G. acaulis (Zone 3, 4"–6"×12") is the famed mountain gentian of southern Europe. It makes low mounds of inch-long leaves above which it bears large, deep sky-blue flowers in early to midspring. Regrettably, it is finicky in gardens, blooming freely in one location and not at all nearby. It seems to want a moist, but gritty, well-drained soil free of lime. It requires sun, but needs shelter from the hottest afternoon sun. Its beauty is worth every effort.
Cultural information: Provide gentians with a rich acid to neutral soil high in leaf mold. Plant them in a bright location where they will be shaded from hot sun.

Geranium cinereum (jir-AY-nee-um sin-AIR-ee-um) **hardy geranium,** LSP-ESU ○ ◐
Zone: 5
Size: 6" × 12"
Native to: Mountains of S. Europe
Uses: Rock garden, alpine meadow, wall, scree, trough
Characteristics: These "true" geraniums are hardy garden plants, as opposed to the tender "bedding" geraniums. Only the smaller kinds are suitable for rock gardens. *G. cinereum* is a bushy plant with grayish green palmate leaves. The pale pink flowers have more deeply colored veins. 'Ballerina' is a form with lilac-pink flowers. *G. c. subcaulescens* bears magenta flowers with a black-purple center. 'Splendens' is reddish purple.
Related species: G. dalmaticum (Dalmatia, Montenegro, Albania, Zone 3, 6"–18") is a charming, dwarf bushy plant with pale pink flowers. *G. d. album* has white flowers. *G. renardii* (Caucasus, Zone 5, 12"×15") has pale pink flowers veined with red and grayer, more velvety foliage than other species. *G. sanguineum striatum* (*G. s. lancastriense*) (Britain, Zone 3, 6×8") is variable in size, but the smaller kinds make excellent, easy to grow rock garden plants.
Cultural information: A well-drained gritty soil is required for *G. renardii* and *G. cinereum*. *G. cinereum* will tolerate lime. *G. renardii* is best planted in a crevice for fast drainage. *G. dalmaticum* and *G. sanguineum*

Gentiana septemfida *var.* latifolia

Geranium cinereum 'Ballerina'

are easily satisfied with an ordinary soil and are less drought tolerant. They prefer partial shade.

Globe daisy; see *Globularia*

Globularia cordifolia

Gypsophila repens

Helianthemum nummularium

Globularia cordifolia
(glob-ew-LAR-ee-a cor-dee-FOH-lee-a)
globe daisy, SU ○ ◑
Zone: 5
Size: 5" × 12"
Native to: Europe
Uses: Rock garden, alpine meadow, wall, scree, trough
Characteristics: These perennials or subshrubs form creeping mats of small leaves that root as they spread. Short stems carry fuzzy rounded heads of pale blue flowers.
Cultural information: Easily grown in ordinary soil, but do best in a scree with full sun, where they can sprawl on stones.

Golden cinquefoil; see ***Potentilla***

Goldenrod; see ***Solidago***

Grass-leaf scabious; see ***Scabiosa***

Gypsophila repens (Jip-SA-fil-a ray-penz) **creeping gypsophila,** SU ○
Zone: 4
Size: 6" × 18"
Native to: Mountains of C. and S. Europe
Uses: Rock garden, alpine meadow, wall, scree, trough
Characteristics: Mats of creeping stems with gray-green foliage provide a background for numerous, showy white to pale pink flowers on these perennials or subshrubs. 'Rosea' has rose-pink flowers.
Related species: G. cerastioides (Himalayas, Zone 5, 2"×10") is a smaller plant for troughs and screes with loose clusters of white flowers above a mound of velvety leaves.

Cultural information: Requires good drainage and prefers, but does not require, lime in the soil.

Hardy geranium; see ***Geranium***

Helianthemum nummularium (heel-ee-AN-the-mum new-mew-LAR-ee-um) rockrose, LSP-ESU ○
Zone: 5
Size: 6" × 24"
Native to: Europe, Asia Minor, N. Africa
Uses: Rock garden, alpine meadow, wall, scree, trough
Characteristics: These low, mat-forming evergreen perennials or subshrubs are highly hybridized and much valued for their range of pastel colors, including yellow, apricot, orange, pink, red and white. The flowers may be either double or single. Some have very gray foliage, others are green.
Cultural information: Although normally evergreen, *H. nummularium* may kill back to the ground in severe winters but will still flower on new growth in summer. Lay evergreen branches over the plants for winter protection in cold regions. Good drainage and an open site are essential to prevent rots; otherwise they are easy to grow, preferring a lean soil. Shear lighly after bloom is finished for a possible repeat performance.

Hen and chickens; see ***Sempervivum***

Houseleek; see ***Sempervivum***

Hypericum cerastoides

Iberis sempervirens
'Purity'

Hypericum cerastoides

(high-PER-ee-kum ser-as-TOY-deez) **St.-John's-wort,** MSU ○

Zone: 6

Size: 6" × 18"

Native to: Bulgaria to Turkey

Uses: Rock garden, wall, scree

Characteristics: The St.-John's-worts are a very useful and adaptable group of plants from different continents. Some are perennials and some shrubs, but all have bright yellow flowers. *H. cerastoides (H. rhodopeum)* is a mat-forming perennial with silvery green foliage. It is too strong a grower for small rock gardens, but striking when spilling out of a wall.

Cultural information: These are easy-to-grow rock plants like good drainage and a warm location among rocks.

Iberis sempervirens

(I-bear-ys sem-pir-VY-renz) **candy-tuft,** SP ○

Zone: 4

Size: 6"–12" × 12"–18"

Native to: S. Europe

Uses: Rock garden, wall, scree, trough

Characteristics: Candytuft is an old-fashioned favorite. Dense mounds of deep, narrow foliage are covered with white flowers. These evergreen perennials or subshrubs are variable in size, and only the smaller types, such as 'Little Gem' (6"×10"), are suitable for small rock gardens and troughs. 'Autumn Snow' may put on a show again in autumn.

Cultural information: Easy to grow in any reasonably well-drained soil in an open location.

Iris pumila

(IR-ys PEW-me-la) **dwarf bearded iris,** ESP ○ ◑

Zone: 4

Size: 6" × 12"

Native to: S.E. Europe to Turkey

Uses: Rock garden, alpine meadow, trough

Characteristics: A miniature of the familiar tall bearded iris. Flowers are well displayed above short, narrow green foliage before the foliage reaches full size. Cultivars and hybrids are available in a range that includes almost every color.

Related species: I. setosa canadensis (E. North America, Zone 2, 6"–8"×10") is a charming dwarf of slighter appearance with narrower leaves and smaller flowers. It is an easy variety with grassy foliage and lavender-blue flowers in late spring. *I. tectorum* (China, Zone 6, 12"–15"×18"), roof iris, is somewhat larger with arching, wide foliage and lilac-blue flowers in midspring. 'Album' is white with yellow crests.

Cultural information: Easy to grow in most garden soils with reasonable drainage. *I. tectorum* is drought tolerant but needs a richer soil than the others.

Jasmine, rock; see ***Androsace***

Iris tectorum 'Album'
(see I. pumila*)*

Lewisia cotyledon

Lychnis flos-jovis minor

Papaver alpinum

Lewisia cotyledon (lew-YSS-ee-a cot-y-LEE-don) **lewisia, SP, ESU** ◑
Zone: 5
Size: 12" × 8"
Native to: N.W. California and S.W. Oregon
Uses: Wall, scree, trough
Characteristics: Of all alpine plants, the evergreen lewisias are among the most cherished and sought after. Even the most beautiful rock garden plants cannot surpass the showy flower clusters in delicate pastel shades of pink, yellow, apricot, salmon-orange and rose. Yet lewisias are not for the novice; they require great skill and careful placement in order to grow successfully. *L. cotyledon* is the easiest species, with rosettes of long, bright green, succulent leaves from which rise multi-branched flower clusters.
Cultural information: Lewisias are highly susceptible to rot in the succulent rosettes and thick, fleshy roots. Provide a very gritty, well-drained, rich soil, high in leaf mold and free of lime. Mulch with deep gravel around the crown, or ideally, plant them on their side in a wall, where no water can sit. A cool eastern or bright northern exposure suits them best. The most successful means of culture is in an alpine house, where they have the longest bloom season.

Lychnis flos-jovis minor (LIK-nys flos-joh-vys migh-nor) **dwarf flower-of-Jove,** SP-ESU ○ ◑
Zone: 4
Size: 8" × 6"
Native to: Europe
Uses: Rock garden, alpine meadow, scree, trough
Characteristics: This is a refined dwarf form of the species in both size and color. Little rosettes of woolly, gray leaves give rise to clusters of clear pink flowers.
Cultural information: Easily grown in the rock garden where it should be allowed to reseed itself.

Meadow rue; see ***Thalictrum***

Mint, Corsican; see ***Mentha***

Moss pink; see ***Phlox***

Onion, flowering; see ***Allium senescens glaucum***

Papaver alpinum (pa-PAY-ver al-PY-num) **alpine poppy,** LSP-SU ○
Zone: 4
Size: 6"–8" × 8"
Native to: European mountains
Uses: Rock garden, alpine meadow, scree, trough
Characteristics: Miniature poppy flowers of white, clear pink, soft yellow and pale orange flutter above ferny gray foliage. Alpine poppies will naturalize themselves in your rock garden, filling empty spaces and creating welcome associations with other plants.
Cultural information: Sow seed where you want the plants to grow because they are virtually impossible to transplant. The individual plants are short-lived, lasting at most three years, but reseed themselves freely.

Pasque flower; see ***Pul-satilla***

Pearlwort; see ***Sagina***

Penstemon davidsonii

(PEN-stem-on day-vid-SON-ee-i) **beard-tongue,** SP-SU ○
Zone: 3
Size: 4" × 18"
Native to: British Columbia to Oregon
Uses: Rock garden, wall, scree, trough
Characteristics: Purple trumpet-shaped flowers rise above a low mat of green foliage. The mat roots as it spreads to form a groundcover.
Related species: P. hirsutus pygmaeus (E. North America, Zone 4, 4"×12") is one of the easiest to grow with short spikes of lavender-blue flowers with white tongues. *P. menziesii* (British Columbia to Washington, zones 6"–7", 6"–8"×15") is actually a shrub with small leaves and large purple flowers. *P. pinifolius* (New Mexico to Mexico, Zone 4, 6"×15") differs in its fine-textured, needlelike foliage and spikes of small tubular scarlet flowers. It likes a dry location but a rich soil.
Cultural information: The beard-tongues require well-drained, gritty, acid soils and resent overwatering, which often kills them. Most prefer a site that faces away from the full force of the afternoon sun.

Persian candytuft; see ***Aethionema***

Phlox subulata

(flocks SUB-ew-lay-ta) **moss pink,** ESP ○ ◐
Zone: 3

Size: 4" × 18"
Native to: New York to Maryland and Michigan
Uses: Rock garden, alpine meadow, wall, scree, trough, path
Characteristics: Colorful mats of the evergreen moss pinks on banks and in walls are a familiar sight in gardens. *P. subulata* has stiff, needlelike, even prickly foliage that is almost obscured by the abundance of pink, coral, red, white, lavender or blue flowers. *P. s. brittonii* is especially desirable for the rock garden with its tight growth habit and white or light pink flowers.
Related species: 'Coral Eye' (6"×18") has white flowers highlighted by a coral center. 'Millstream Juniper' bears lovely deep blue flowers. Both are hybrids created by Lincoln Foster at Millstream, his Connecticut rock garden.
Cultural information: The moss pinks are easy to grow in most well-drained soils, but a lean, stony, neutral to alkaline soil suits these plants best.

Pink, Cheddar; See Dianthus

Poppy, alpine; see ***Papaver***

Potentilla aurea

(poh-ten-TIL-a OR-ree-a) **golden cinquefoil,** SP ○ ◐
Zone: 5
Size: 4"–6" × 8"
Native to: Europe
Uses: Rock garden, alpine meadow, trough, path
Characteristics: This is one of the most popular dwarf cinquefoils suitable for rock gardens.

Penstemon menziesii
(see P. davidsonii*)*

Phlox subulata *'Coral Eye'*

Potentilla tridentata *'Minima'* (see P. aurea)

Tight clumps or mats of small, five-parted, deep green leaves produce golden yellow flowers. *Related species: P. alba* (E. Europe, Zone 5, 10"×12") has larger silver-haired leaves and white flowers with a yellow center from early spring into summer. *P. cinerea* (C., S. and E. Europe, Zone 5, 2"×10") has silvery leaves and bright yellow flowers on creeping stems in spring. *P. tridentata* 'Minima' (E. North America, Zone 2, 6"×12") creeps through walls and as a groundcover by means of shallow underground rhizomes. It makes a mat of dark green three-parted leaves, each tipped with three teeth. The white flowers are held in loose branched clusters in early summer. Some leaves take on red autumn color, while others remain evergreen.

Cultural information: Most cinquefoils like a rich, moist soil and are not as demanding of fast drainage as are so many other rock garden plants. *P. cinerea*, however, does require stoney conditions and good drainage. *P. tridentata* will take part shade.

Primrose; see *Primula*

Primula auricula (PRIM-ew-la or-IK-ew-la) **primrose**, SP ◑

Zone: 3
Size: 8" × 8"
Native to: Mountains of Europe
Uses: Rock garden, alpine meadow, wall, scree, trough
Characteristics: No discussion of rock gardening would be complete without primroses. There are hundreds of species

throughout the world, with many native to Europe and Asia. Except in cool alpine or northern climates, primroses are not suited to growing in sun. Often they are found in the lee of rocks with bright light and partial shade. At lower elevations they inhabit woodlands and moist areas. The alpine species are true rock plants, many preferring scree and moraine conditions. They resent hot weather and excess moisture around the roots and crown. *P. auricula* is the best known species and has many variations and relatives throughout the European mountains. The species and its numerous hybrids are frequently referred to simply as "auriculas." Farina, an attractive waxy meal, often coats the succulent leaves and stems. The flowers are held in clusters on stocky stems. The hybrids in particular are beautifully marked as if painted with bright colors of yellow, red and green.

Related species: P. × *pubescens* is an often grown hybrid auricula. *P. vulgaris* (*P. acaulis*) and the showier hybrid *P.* × *polyantha* varieties are easier to grow under normal garden conditions and are easily obtained. They are available in nearly every color, including yellow, pink, salmon, red, white and blue.

Cultural information: The auriculas require rocky, well-drained soils, preferably neutral to alkaline, which simulate the rocky limestone soils of their native habitats. At low altitudes, provide light shade, especially during the heat of day. Planting on a bank or directly in a wall

seems to suit them best in the garden. They are easier to grow in alpine houses and well suited to troughs. *P. vulgaris* and *P.* × *polyantha* are more easily grown in a moist soil, rich in leaf mold. They are better suited to low elevations, but need part shade and shelter from extreme heat. The commonly sold large flowered hybrids are characteristically short-lived; more perennial strains should be sought from specialist nurseries for garden use.

Pulsatilla vulgaris (pul-sa-TIL-la vul-GAR-is) **pasque flower**, ESP ○ ◑

Zone: 5
Size: 10" × 12"
Native to: Europe
Uses: Rock garden, alpine meadow, scree
Characteristics: Silky buds emerge early in the season, opening to purple flowers with yellow stamens, which are followed by deeply and finely cut leaves. 'Alba' and 'Rubra' have white and ruby red flowers, respectively.

Cultural information: Pasque flowers need a reasonably well-drained rock garden soil, but are otherwise one of the easier plants to grow. They usually grow in limey soils. Established plants have deep roots and do not transplant well.

Purple rock cress; see *Aubrieta*

Pussytoes; see *Antennaria*

Rock cress; see *Arabis*

Rock cress, purple; see *Aubrieta*

Primula × polyantha
'Dwarf Jewel'
(see P. auricula)

Pulsatilla vulgaris

Sagina subulata (*grown in pots*)

Rock jasmine; see ***Andro-sace***

Rockfoil; see ***Saxifraga***

Rockrose; see ***Helianthe-mum***

Rue, meadow; see ***Thali-ctrum***

Sagina subulata (sa-JY-na SUB-ew-lay-ta) **pearlwort,** SU
○
Zone: 4
Size: 2" × 10"
Native to: Europe
Uses: Rock garden, alpine meadow, wall, scree, trough, path
Characteristics: Pearlwort makes a very fine-textured, low-creep- ing mound dusted with tiny white flowers. This evergreen is ideal for planting in paths among stones but is too inva- sive and competitive to be planted among other small rock garden plants. 'Aurea' has golden foliage.
Cultural information: Pearlworts will not tolerate hot or droughty locations and are ideal for low, poorly drained paths.

Saponaria ocymoides

Sandwort; see *Arenaria*

Saponaria ocymoides (sa-pon-AIR-ee-a o-sy-MOY-deez) **soap-wort,** SU ○
Zone: 4
Size: 6" × 24"
Native to: Mountains of S. Europe
Uses: Rock garden, wall, scree
Characteristics: This soapwort forms a sprawling, loose mat of dark green foliage with lavender-pink flowers, that is perhaps best hanging out of a wall. *S. o.* 'Rubra Compacta' is an improved, compact variety with deeper pink flowers.
Related species: S. caespitosa (Pyrenees, Zone 7, 6"×6") makes a low, tight mound with pink flowers. *S.* × *lempergii* 'Max Frei' (Zone 6, 6"–12"×18") is a hybrid with deep pink flowers in late summer and slightly gray foliage.
Cultural information: Soapworts are easy to grow in a gritty, well-drained soil. *S. caespitosa* likes a limey soil.

Saxifraga paniculata (saks-ee-FRAY-ja pan-y-ku-LAY-ta) **rockfoil,** ESU ◑
Zone: 2
Size: 10" × 4"
Native to: Europe, Asia, N. America
Uses: Rock garden, wall, trough
Characteristics: The saxifrages present one of the ultimate challenges and temptations to rock gardeners. The most beautiful kinds are the mossy and kabschia types with tight buns of mounded foliage and masses of tiny flowers in a full range of delicate colors, including white, primrose-yellow, pink, apricot and purple. These evergreens are not for the novice, requiring a cool climate, skill and preferably an alpine house. The encrusted types are much easier to grow and many are suitable for rock garden conditions. They are so named for the encrustations of lime, secreted along the leaf margins. *S. paniculata* (*S. aizoon*) is typical of the encrusted group with 2- to 3-inch rosettes. From these arise branched stems, up to 10 inches tall, with numerous white, yellow or pink flowers. The older rosettes die after they bloom, but are replaced by their offshoots clustered around the base. *S. paniculata* will form colonies or spread through walls.
Related species: S. cotyledon (Europe, North America, Zone 6, 28"×3"–5"), is also an encrusted type. It is larger with white flowers, which are sometimes veined or spotted with red.
Cultural information: Almost all rockfoils require gritty soils with good drainage, but also suffer from drought. Many (not including *S. cotyledon*) prefer lime. They sulk in hot weather, so except in cool climates, they must be sheltered from hot midday sun. They do, however, require bright light.

Saxifraga cotyledon *(see S. paniculata)*

Scabiosa graminifolia

Scabiosa graminifolia

(SKA-bee-oh-sa gram-in-i-FOL-ee-a) **grass-leaf scabious,** SU ◯

Zone: 6
Size: 10" × 12"
Native to: S. Europe
Uses: Rock garden, alpine meadow, wall, scree
Characteristics: A long blooming plant with long, narrow, silvery leaves and lavender-blue flowers.
Related species: S. lucida (C. Europe, Zone 5, 8×10") has rose-lilac-colored flowers.
Cultural information: Easy to grow in a reasonably drained soil, where they will reseed themselves.

Scabious, grass-leaf; see *Scabiosa*

Sea pink; see *Armeria*

Sedge; see *Carex*

Sedum dasyphyllum (SEE-

dum day-see-FIL-um **stonecrop,** SP ◯ ◑

Zone: 4
Size: 4" × 20"

Native to: Europe, N. Africa
Uses: Rock garden, alpine meadow, wall, scree, trough
Characteristics: The stonecrops are a variable group. Some are too large or invasive to associate with dwarf rock plants, but many of these evergreen perennials are dependable survivors with good habits. *S. dasyphyllum* makes a slowly growing low mat of ovoid gray-blue leaves and white flowers flushed with pink.
Related Species: S. cauticola (Japan, Zone 3, 5"×8") forms a slowly spreading clump with rounded gray leaves and heads of rose-pink flowers in late summer and autumn. *S. sieboldii* (Japan, Zone 4, 10"–12"× 18"–24") is similar to *S. cauticola,* but has larger leaves, longer horizontal stems and flowers later in autumn. Both are best displayed in walls. One of the commonest species in gardens is *S. spurium* (Caucasus, Zone 4, 4"×18"), but it spreads too rapidly and can quickly take over all but the largest rock gardens. *S.* 'Vera

Sedum dasyphyllum

Jameson' (Zone 3, 6"–9"×12") is a fine hybrid clump-former with grayish plum-colored leaves and heads of rose-pink flowers in late summer. It is one of the best.
Cultural information: The stonecrops are some of the toughest rock garden plants for exposed, dry sunny places. They seem to thrive in any ordinary or poor soil, provided it is not waterlogged. *S. sieboldii* is especially attractive to slugs.

Sempervivum

Sempervivum spp. and hybrids (sem-pir-VIGH-vum) **hen and chickens, houseleek,** SU ○ ◑

Zones: 4–5
Size: 9"–12" × 6"
Native to: Europe and N. Africa
Uses: Rock garden, wall, scree, trough
Characteristics: The evergreen hen and chickens are such a diverse group that to single out specific kinds as the best would be of little help to gardeners. Instead, I recommend you choose those that appeal to you most at your local nursery. A varied selection is usually available. The succulent rosettes range in size from under 1 inch to more than 6 inches in shades of green, pink, red, purple or even silvery gray. Many are multicolored and some are downy or studded with cobwebby hairs connecting the tips of the segments. The oldest rosettes extend into a flower stalk with green to yellow, pink, purple or even salmon flowers before they die

and are replaced by adjacent offsets.
Related species: S. *arachnoideum* (mountains of S. Europe, Zone 5, 4"–12"×1–2") has small rosettes with striking cobwebs. It will cling to the face of a moisture-retentive rock with its tiny roots. Flowers are rose to salmon-pink. S. *tectorum* (C. Europe, Zone 4, 12"×4") seems to be the most common in gardens, possibly due to its tough constitution. It has large olive-green rosettes. The many *Sempervivum* species and hundreds of hybrids with mixed-up names confuse even the most accomplished botanists.
Cultural information: Sempervivums are among the most recognized and grown rock plants. They are remarkable for their ability to thrive in the tiniest crevice or pocket of poor soil, and to withstand considerable drought. What they do demand is good drainage in a sandy or gritty soil or atop a wall, to keep from rotting. They look their most radiant in spring

when the weather is cool and moist. They are ideally suited to growing between the stones in walls where they will increase into dense colonies. Divide and replant young rosettes in spring or summer when they become very crowded.

Silene schafta (sigh-LEE-nee SHAF-ta) **campion, catchfly,** SU-F ○

Zone: 4
Size: 10" × 6"
Native to: Caucasus
Uses: Rock garden, alpine meadow, scree, trough
Characteristics: An especially useful alpine for late summer bloom, particularly for novice gardeners, because it is easy to grow. Tufted rosettes of hairy, light green leaves give rise to thin stems with rose-magenta flowers.
Related species: S. *alpestris* (mountains of S. Europe, Zone 5, 8"×18") has glossy leaves and white, fringed blossoms. The flowers of 'Flore-Pleno' are double with extra petals.

Silene alpestris *'Flore-Pleno' (see* S. schafta)

Cultural information: Despite their dwarf stature, the easiest campions are remarkably simple to grow in ordinary soil. *S. alpestris* requires better drainage and prefers some lime. They are short-lived perennials or biennials, so should be permitted to self-sow.

Soapwort; see *Saponaria*

Solidago cutleri (sol-y-DAY-go CUT-ler-i) **goldenrod**, LSU ○
Zone: 4
Size: 4"–14" × 12"
Native to: mountains of E. N. America
Uses: Rock gardens, alpine meadow, wall, scree, trough
Characteristics: Many goldenrods make exceptionally beautiful garden plants in spite of the prejudice directed toward them. It is a myth that they cause hay fever. Several dwarf species make easy rock plants for late summer and autumn bloom. *S. cutleri* forms clumps of large leaves with tight clusters of bright yellow flowers on short stems.
Related species: S. virgaurea minutissima (Japan, Zone 5, 4"×4") is a particularly dwarf goldenrod, and one of the few not native to North America.
Cultural information: Goldenrods are tough plants that are satisfied with ordinary garden soil but maintain a dwarfer habit in a poor soil. They are easy plants that should be tried by all beginners.

Speedwell; see *Veronica*

St.-John's-wort; see *Hypericum cerastoides*

Stone cress; see *Aethionema*

Stonecrop; see *Sedum*

Thalictrum coreanum
(THAL-eek-trum kor-ee-AY-num) **meadow rue**, SP ◑
Zone: 4
Size: 8" × 12"
Native to: N. Asia
Uses: Rock garden, alpine meadow, wall, trough
Characteristics: Clusters of spherical lavender-pink flowers dance above small rounded leaflets on wiry stems, similar to columbine. Also known as *T. ichangense.*
Related species: T. kiusianum (Japan, Zone 5, 6"×10") is similar and spreads somewhat by rhizomes.
Cultural information: Meadow rues are not for the dry exposed conditions favored by many rock plants. They prefer a sheltered location in partial shade with rich, moist, acid soil, but will tolerate more sun if the soil remains moist.

Thrift; see *Armeria*

Veronica incana (ver-ON-ee-ka in-KAN-a) **speedwell**, LSP-ESU ○
Zone: 3
Size: 12"–18" × 18"
Native to: Russia
Uses: Rock garden, alpine meadow, wall
Characteristics: Low mats of silvery foliage produce long lax flower spikes with deep blue flowers that open over a long period.
Related species: V. austraica teucrium 'Shirley Blue' (Europe, Zone 3, 8"×15") is a bushy spreading plant with deep green foliage. When in bloom it is covered with short, deep blue spikes. 'Trehane' (6"×15"), an unusual cultivar with golden foliage and deep blue flowers, prefers a little shade (or the foliage may burn). *V. oltensis* (on rocky cliffs in Turkey, Zone 4, 2"×12") creeps between rocks to form a low mat with tiny gray-green leaves and short spikes of light

Solidago virgaurea
(see S. cutleri)

Thalictrum coreanum

Veronica oltensis *(see* V. incana*)*

blue flowers. *V. prostrata* (*V. rupestris*) (Europe, Zone 5, 3"×18") is an excellent creeping groundcover with short, deep blue spikes. There are also white and pink flowered forms. *V. stelleri* (Japan, Zone 5, 3"–6"×8") is another low plant with hairy leaves and blue flower spikes. *V.* 'Goodness Grows' (Zone 3, 10"–12"×20") is a sprawling, unrefined hybrid too vigorous for very small rock gardens. It flowers from spring to late fall with deep blue flowers and bright green foliage.

Cultural information: Compared to many rock garden plants, the demands of the speedwells are simple. They want an ordinary garden soil with reasonable drainage and full or nearly full sun. *V. incana* requires a drier, more open location to prevent rot.

Woolly yarrow; see *Achillea*

Yarrow, woolly; see *Achillea*

BULBS

Allium oreophilum (AL-lee-um or-ee-oh-FIL-um) **flowering onion,** LSP ○
Zone: 4
Size: 4" × 4"
Native to: Turkestan to C. Asia
Uses: Rock garden, alpine meadow, scree, trough
Characteristics: The bulbous onions are a varied group with both very tall and very dwarf species. This is one of the prettiest little ones with clusters of rose-pink flowers held above two long, straplike leaves.

Cultural information: After flowering, this onion will die down and become dormant for the summer. Provide a location in well-drained soil that can be allowed to dry out in summer. The foliage has an oniony scent when bruised. Plant 4 to 5 inches deep.

Anemone blanda (an-e-MOH-ne BLAN-da) **Greek windflower, anemone,** ESP-MSP ○ ◑
Zone: 4
Size: 4" × 4"
Native to: Greece, E. Europe
Uses: Rock garden, alpine meadow
Characteristics: Blue, white or pink flowers, composed of many narrow petals, open on warm sunny days above dark green, finely cut foliage. Not a true bulb, this is actually a rhizome.

Cultural information: These windflowers require a well-drained site, preferably in a rich soil where they can dry out during their summer dormancy. Plant 4 inches deep.

Allium oreophilum

Anemone blanda

Colchicum *'Lilac Wonder' (see* C. autumnale*)*

Crocus chrysanthus *'E.A. Bowles'*

Colchicum autumnale

(COL-chee-cum aw-tum-NAL-ee) **col-chicum, meadow saffron,** EF ○ ◑
Zone: 5
Size: 8" × 24"
Native to: Europe
Uses: Rock garden, alpine meadow
Characteristics: Pink or white crocuslike flowers emerge in autumn without leaves. The leaves follow in spring, die down in June and remain dormant for the summer. *C. autumnale* has smaller foliage than most other species and hybrids, which makes it more suitable for the rock garden. Even so, the foliage of these corms is likely to smother small plants nearby.
Related species: C. byzantinum is one of the earliest, blooming in late summer, and most floriferous but has some of the largest leaves. There are many hybrids: 'Princess Astrid' is early, with deep lavender-pink, checkered flowers. 'Lilac Wonder' is also very floriferous and the last to bloom with rich pink flowers.

Cultural information: Colchicum are adaptable to a wide range of soils, including clay. The flowers are attractive to slugs, but the bulbs are very poisonous and will be left alone by other animals. Plant 6 inches deep.

Coral lily; see *Lilium*

Crocus chrysanthus (KRO-kus kry-SAN-thus) **snow crocus,** LW-ESP ○ ◑ ⑪
Zone: 4
Size: 4"–6" × 4"
Native to: E. Europe, Asia Minor
Uses: Rock garden, alpine meadow, scree, trough
Characteristics: The small snow crocuses are highly valued for their very early bloom and clear colors. The yellow, white or blue flowers with yellow centers are sometimes attractively marked on the outside. They open on warm days and close at night. Narrow, grasslike foliage appears with the flowers. These are actually corms, not true bulbs.

Related species: C. vernus hybrids, the Dutch crocuses, are larger and later blooming, but lack the delicacy of color. Fall blooming species resemble the spring bloomers, but many bloom without their foliage: *C. speciosus* (E. Europe to W. Asia, Zone 4, 4"–6"×4") is the easiest fall-blooming species to grow, but may become weedy in the rock garden. Flowers appear in October in shades of lavender-blue or white with prominent orange stigmas in the center. *C. kotschyanus* (*C. zonatus*) (Turkey to Lebanon, Zone 5, 4"–6"×4") is lavender, with a golden throat, and is less weedy. *C. goulimyi* (S. Greece, Zone 7, 6"×4") produces leaves along with its lilac flowers.
Cultural information: Any well-drained soil will suit crocuses, but they are a favorite food of mice, voles and squirrels. A very gravelly soil helps to discourage animals. Plant 3 to 4 inches deep.

Daffodil; see *Narcissus*

Fritillaria michailovskyi

Galanthus nivalis

Iris reticulata 'Cantab'

suited to the rock garden because of its size, bright color and adaptability to rock garden conditions. Nodding yellow and purplish red flowers hang atop straight stems.
Cultural information: Provide a well-drained, gritty soil and allow to dry out in summer when plants are dormant. Plant 4 inches deep.

Fritillary; see *Fritillaria*

Galanthus nivalis (gal-AN-thus ny-VAL-is) **snowdrop,** LW-ESP ○ ◑ ⦿
Zone: 3
Size: 6" × 4"
Native to: Europe
Uses: Rock garden, alpine meadow, scree, trough
Characteristics: The nodding white flowers of snowdrops are among the first winter or spring flowers.
Cultural information: Snowdrops are easily satisfied by most garden soils and they do not require a dry period while dormant in summer. Plant 4 inches deep.

Greek windflower; see *Anemone*

Iris reticulata (I-rys ray-TIK-ew-la-ta) **reticulated iris,** ESP ○ ◑ ⦿
Zone: 5
Size: 4"–6" × 4"
Native to: Turkey to Iran
Uses: Rock garden, alpine meadow, trough
Characteristics: Fragrant blue, purple or reddish-purple flowers appear before the leaves, which elongate to a foot longby

Flowering onion; see *Allium oreophilum*

Fritillaria michailovskyi (fri-til-LAR-ee-a mik-ay-LOV-sky-i) **fritillary,** SP ○
Zone: 6
Size: 9" × 6"
Native to: Turkey
Uses: Rock garden, alpine meadow, scree, trough
Characteristics: This newly available fritillary is ideally

late spring, when they go dormant.
Related species: I. danfordiae (Turkey, Zone 5, 4"–6"×4") is yellow and seldom blooms after the first year, but new bulbs are inexpensive.
Cultural information: I. reticulata will multiply and flower for years in a well-drained rock garden without competition from tree roots. *I. danfordiae* may be encouraged to persist if planted more than 6 inches deep in a very well-drained, dry location. Plant 4 inches deep.

Lilium pumilum (LIL-ee-um PEW-mill-um) **coral lily,** ESU ○ ◑
Zone: 3
Size: 12"–24" × 12"
Native to: N.E. Asia
Uses: Rock garden, alpine meadow
Characteristics: This is the only lily species small and delicate enough to be suitable for most rock gardens. Each plant carries an average of 10 flowers on the top of the stalk. The coral-red petals reflex back strongly for a "Turk's cap"-shaped flower.
Cultural information: Like all other lilies, the coral lily requires a well-drained soil. Plant the bulbs 4 to 5 inches deep. Since individual plants of this species are short-lived (lasting only two to four years), allow them to self-sow, which they will do readily when happy. Plant 6 inches deep.

Lily, coral; see *Lilium*

Meadow saffron; see *Colchicum*

Lilium pumilum

Narcissus *'Tête-à-Tête'*

Narcissus spp. and hybrids (nar-SYS-sus) **daffodil,** MSP ○ ◐ ⦶

Zones: 4"–6
Size: 4"–24" × 4"–8"
Native to: Europe
Uses: Rock garden, alpine meadow
Characteristics: Daffodils scarcely need an introduction, except to advise that you only plant the dwarf hybrids and species, under 12 inches, in your rock garden. There are many to choose from. Not only will the larger kinds look out of scale, but their large foliage will be unsightly for a few months after bloom and may smother small plants nearby. Some fine dwarfs to watch for are: 'Baby Moon'— 4 inches, golden yellow; 'Jack Snipe'—8 inches, white petals with a long yellow trumpet; 'Little Gem'—4 inches, a charming golden yellow miniature trumpet daffodil; 'Tête-à-Tête'—6 inches, clusters of yellow flowers.
Cultural information: Almost any soil with reasonable drainage and organic matter will suit the majority of daffodil varieties. In very hot summer climates of southern regions, they

need a shaded location to keep the soil cool during summer. Plant 4 to 6 inches deep depending on variety. Seldom bothered by animals.

Onion, flowering; see ***Allium oreophilum***

Reticulated iris; see ***Iris reticulata***

Saffron, meadow; see ***Colchicum***

Snow crocus; see ***Crocus***

Snowdrop; see ***Galanthus***

Tulip; see ***Tulipa***

Tulipa tarda (TEW-li-pa TAR-da) **tulip,** MSP ○
Zone: 4
Size: 4" × 4"
Native to: Turkestan
Uses: Rock garden, alpine meadow
Characteristics: Many of the dwarf species tulips are ideally suited to the rock garden, where they may settle down happily in well-drained soils and last for many years. *T. tarda* (*T. dasystemon*) is one of the easiest to grow and may even

seed itself. It has yellow flowers edged with white that open wide in the sun and close at night.
Related species: T. batalinii (C. Asia, Zone 4, 4"–6"×5") has light yellow, cup-shaped flowers, sometimes flushed with apricot. *T. chrysantha* (Iran, N.W. India, Zone 6, 8"×4") is tall and slender, the flowers are red, margined with yellow. *T. linifolia* (C. Asia, Zone 4) has striking bright red flowers with a black center that is prominently displayed in the sun. *T. humilis* (*T. pulchella, T. violacea*) (Turkey to Iran, Zone 5, 4"–6"×5") are often called crocus tulips because of their early spring bloom and similar size. They vary from shades of pink to lavender and violet with a yellow or black center.
Cultural information: Tulips require good drainage and a fertile soil in order to do their best. They prefer a dry, hot soil while dormant in summer. Plant them deep, from 6 to 12 inches, to encourage longevity. They may be eaten by mice, voles, rabbits, squirrels and deer.

Windflower, Greek; see ***Anemone***

Tulipa tarda

SHRUBS

Bearberry willow; see *Salix*

Broom; see *Genista*

Broom, prostrate; see *Cytisus*

Calluna vulgaris (Ka-LEW-na vul-GA-ris) **heather,** LSU ○ ◑

Zone: 4
Size: 4"–20" × 24"
Native to: Europe, Asia Minor
Uses: Rock garden, alpine meadow, wall
Characteristics: Heathers are low, procumbent evergreen shrubs closely related to the heaths with very fine-textured, needlelike foliage. The small bell-shaped flowers are deep pink, lavender-pink or white.
Cultural information: Heathers need a well-drained acid soil high in organic matter, but of low fertility to prevent rangy growth. Trim branches in spring, before growth starts, to promote compactness.

Cotoneaster microphyllus thymifolius (co-TOH-nee-as-ter my-kroh-FIL-us ty-mi-FOL-ee-us) **cotoneaster,** SP ○ ◑
Zone: 5
Size: 12" × 2"
Native to: Himalaya
Uses: Rock garden, scree, trough
Characteristics: This is the smallest cotoneaster and is ideal for planting among other wee plants or in a trough. This evergreen shrub forms a low mound with tiny, deep green leaves and tiny white flowers, which are followed by red berries in fall. *Cotoneaster Microphyllus* 'Cochleatus' is also excellent for rock gardens, but it is not quite as dwarf as *C.m. thymifolius*, and therefore not as suitable for troughs.
Cultural information: Cotoneasters are not difficult to grow in most well-drained soils. In hot climates, provide this one with shelter from the hottest sun and avoid drought.

Cytisus decumbens (sy-TIS-sus DEE-cum-benz) **prostrate broom,** SP ○
Zone: 5
Size: 6" × 12"
Native to: S.E. Europe
Uses: Rock garden, alpine meadow, wall, scree, trough
Characteristics: Bright yellow, pea-shaped flowers cover this low mounded evergreen shrub in May and June. Though the leaves are somewhat sparse, the green stems are quite attractive.
Cultural information: The brooms are adapted to dry, well-drained, infertile soils. They're easy to grow if given an open situation with plenty of sun. They are difficult to transplant successfully so should only be planted as small potted plants.

Daphne cneorum (DAF-nee nee-OR-um) **daphne,** SP ○ ◑
Zone: 5
Size: 6"–12" × 24"
Native to: Mountains of Europe

Calluna vulgaris

Cotoneaster microphyllus 'Cochleatus'

Cytisus decumbens

Uses: Rock garden, alpine meadow, wall, scree, trough
Characteristics: Daphnes are some of the most fragrant shrubs. Virtually all of these evergreens are suitable for rock gardens, although the larger kinds may outgrow their space and cannot be transplanted successfully. *D. cneorum* is a low prostrate species with pink or white flowers. *D. cneurum* 'Variegata' has leaves edged with yellow. Many varieties are available, but 'Eximia' has proven to be one of the most reliable and easiest to grow.
Related species: D. × mantensiana (Zone 6, 24"×24") is a hybrid bearing lavender-purple flowers all summer.
Cultural information: These fickle shrubs have the reputation of dying without cause, even after many years of healthy growth. They are also nearly impossible to transplant and should be planted as small potted plants in a permanent location. Nevertheless, they will grow in most well-drained soils, preferring a near-neutral pH.

Erica carnea (ER-i-ca car-NEE-a) **heath,** LW-ESP ○ ◐

Zone: 4
Size: 12" × 24"
Native to: E. Europe
Uses: Rock garden, alpine meadow
Characteristics: These low-spreading, evergreen shrubs are closely related to the heathers. The stems are lined with short, needlelike foliage and urn-shaped flowers in shades of pink and white.
Related species: E. cinerea (W. Europe, Zone 5, 12"–24"×24") is similar and blooms in summer.

Cultural information: Heaths like an acid soil high in organic matter, but of only moderate fertility to discourage leggy growth. Shear after flowering to encourage a more compact habit.

Genista pilosa (jen-IS-ta pi-LOH-sa) **woadwaxen or broom,** SP-ESU ○ ◐

Zone: 5
Size: 24" × 36"
Native to: Europe
Uses: Rock garden, alpine meadow, wall, scree
Characteristics: Like *Cytisus,* the woadwaxens make stemmy mounds that cover themselves with yellow, pea-shaped flowers. The green stems combine nicely with the gray-green leaves. *G. p.* 'Vancouver Gold' is a vigorous, floriferous cultivar introduced by the University of British Columbia Botanical Garden. It is not appropriate for the small rock garden.
Related species: G. dalmatica (Zone 5, 4"×15") is a better size for small rock gardens and troughs and bears fragrant, butter-yellow flowers in early summer. It is densely twiggy and spiny.
Cultural information: The woadwaxens are tolerant of heat, drought and poor soils. They adapt to either an alkaline or an acid soil as long as it is gritty or sandy and well drained, but they are difficult to transplant once established.

Daphne cneorum 'Variegata'

Erica carnea

Genista pilosa

Hypericum olympicum

Ilex crenata 'Dwarf Pagoda'

Lavandula angusti-
folia 'Munstead'

Heath; see *Erica*

Heather; see *Calluna*

Holly, Japanese; see *Ilex*

Hypericum olympicum
(high-PER-ee-kum   oh-lym-PY-kum)
St.-John's-wort, MSU ○
Zone: 6
Size: 12" × 15"
Native to: S. Europe to Asia
Minor
Uses: Rock garden, wall, scree
Characteristics: The St.-John's-
worts are a very useful and
adaptable group of plants from
different continents. Some of
these deciduous plants are perennials and some shrubs, but
all have bright yellow flowers.
H. olympicum is one of the
finer textured bushy shrubs
with small, rounded, grayish
leaves and an abundance of
flowers at the ends of the
stems. 'Citrina' is a pleasant,
light yellow cultivar that mixes
nicely with plants with harsh
pink flowers.
Related species: H. buckleyi
(mountains of North Carolina
and Georgia, Zone 5, 12"×24")
is a procumbent shrub that
flowers in June.
Cultural information: Easy-to-
grow rock plants that like good
drainage and a warm location
among rocks. Cut back *H.
olympicum* severely in spring
for best performance.

Ilex crenata 'Dwarf Pa-
goda' (I-leks kren-A-ta) **Japanese holly,** SP ○ ◑
Zones: 6–7
Size: 24"–48" × 12"–24"
Native to: Japan
Uses: Rock garden, trough
Characteristics: Japanese hollies range in size from over 10
feet to very dwarf. All have
dark green evergreen foliage.
Only the smallest growing
types are suitable for rock gardens. 'Dwarf Pagoda' with an
upright habit of growth and
picturesque, irregular horizontal branches, may take 10
years to reach 1 foot tall. It is
female and bears black berries
in fall. 'Green Dragon' is a similar, male cultivar. 'Piccolo'
and 'Rock Garden' are among
the slowest growing, remaining
tight, rounded shrubs under 6
inches for many years. All are
very slow growing, but will
grow faster in a richer soil.
Cultural information: Japanese
hollies are easy to grow in almost any well-drained, moderately acid soil.

Japanese holly; see *Ilex*

Lavender; see *Lavandula*

Lavandula angustifolia
(lav-en-DEW-la   an-gust-y-FOL-ee-a)
lavender, SU ○
Zone: 5
Size: 12"–24" × 18"–36"
Native to: S. Europe, N. Africa
Uses: Rock garden, wall, scree

Characteristics: This evergreen plant is the source of the renowned fragrance. Both the flowers and the foliage are aromatic. Foliage may be green, but more commonly gray, which is the best foil for the lavender, purple or sometimes white flower spikes. The smallest cultivars should be selected for the rock garden. 'Nana' (12"×12") is compact with pleasing gray leaves. 'Munstead' (18"×24") is another common dwarf cultivar, originally from the garden of Gertrude Jekyll.

Cultural information: A rock garden is the ideal place to grow lavender because they require dry, well-drained soil. They are happiest with a neutral or alkaline pH. Shear back the plants after flowering or in early spring to keep them from becoming open and leggy. Young plants are most durable and attractive.

Paxistima canbyi (paks-IS-ti-ma KAN-bee-i) **paxistima,** SP ○ ◐

Zone: 3
Size: 12" × 36"
Native to: Mountains of Virginia and West Virginia
Uses: Rock garden, alpine meadow, wall
Characteristics: A durable, spreading evergreen mat of dark green foliage with relatively unshowy reddish flowers.
Cultural information: Paxistima grows wild on a limey soil, but will grow perfectly well on a moderately acid soil that is moist, well drained and enriched with organic matter.

Prostrate broom; see *Cytisus*

Rhododendron racemosum (roh-doh-DEN-dron ra-se-MOH-sum) **rhododendron,** SP ◐

Zone: 5
Size: 12"–60" × 18"–60"
Native to: Japan
Uses: Rock garden, alpine meadow, wall, scree, trough
Characteristics: The rhododendrons are a numerous and varied group of plants. While some of these evergreen shrubs are treelike giants with huge leaves and flowers, many low-growing species with small leaves carpet the high mountain meadows of Europe and Asia, providing a heathlike groundcover. These species and their hybrids find the perfect home in rock gardens. Fortunately, the choice of dwarfs is extensive. A lovely and easy species is *R. racemosum* with masses of small pink buds that open to white flowers edged with pink. Most forms of this rhododendron in gardens are the ideal size, reaching a foot or two in height.

Related species: R. impeditum (W. China, Zone 4, eventually to 36" tall) is the perfect dwarf species for the rock garden with bright purple flowers and a tight compact habit, but it does not endure hot summers well. Some of its purple hybrid progeny are easier to grow. *R. kiusianum* (Japan, Zone 6, to 36" tall) is a dwarf evergreen azalea with tiny leaves and pink or white flowers. *R. yakusimanum* (high mountains of S. Japan, zones 5–6, 36"×36") has become one of the most admired of all rhododendrons with a densely compact habit and larger leaves, to 6 inches

Paxistima canbyi

Rhododendron yakusimanum *'Koichira Wada' (see* R. racemosum)

long. The undersides of the dark green leaves and new growth are covered with a thick, woolly, brown indumentum. Rich pink buds open to thick-petaled white flowers in tight clusters. *R. yakusimanum* has been the parent of many good "yak" hybrids of similar habit and varied flower colors.

The many dwarf hybrid rhododendrons (all with small leaves) include: 'Carmen' with deep red bells, 'Ginny Gee' with pink buds opening to white, 'Patty Bee' with light yellow flowers and 'Small Wonder', which has dark red flowers, and is more heat resistant than many dwarf reds.

Cultural information: Rhododendrons require a moist, acid, organic soil, with good drainage. In hot climates they need partial shade, but will bloom more prolifically in sun.

Salix yesoalpina *(see S. uva-ursi)*

Spiraea bullata

Salix uva-ursi (SAY-liks U-va-UR-sy) **bearberry willow,** ESP ○ ◑
Zone: 2
Size: 2" × 18"
Native to: Arctic region of N. America
Uses: Rock garden, alpine meadow, trough
Characteristics: Many dwarf alpine willows will adapt to lowland rock gardens and charm you with their miniature early spring "pussies" or catkins.
Related species: S. yesoalpina (Japan, Zone 4, 4"×36") is a large-leafed dwarf prostrate willow that will gracefully cascade over a wall or trough.
Cultural information: Since these are alpine or arctic plants, they are best with protection from midday heat and should not be allowed to dry out. They prefer an acid soil well enriched with organic matter, such as leaf mold.

Spiraea bullata (spir-EE-a bu-LAY-ta) **spirea,** SU ○
Zone: 4
Size: 12"–15" × 36"
Native to: E. N. America
Uses: Rock garden, alpine meadow
Characteristics: This deciduous shrub forms a dense mound of

small leaves and heads of pink flowers that bloom all summer. This is a plant that is useful to fill a difficult space or create a transition between the rock garden and another area.
Cultural information: This is an easy plant for any soil in sun.

Spirea; see ***Spiraea***

St.-John's-wort; see ***Hypericum olympicum***

Thyme; see ***Thymus***

Thymus praecox arcticus (TY-mus PRAY-kokz ARK-tee-kus) **thyme,** SU ○
Zone: 4
Size: 1"–2" × 12"–18"
Native to: Europe
Uses: Rock garden, alpine meadow, scree, trough
Characteristics: Thymes are creeping shrubs with small, aromatic leaves. They come from dry, rocky habitats and make well-behaved companions for all except the smallest rock plants. They are ideal groundcovers for the alpine meadow. Many of the low types are especially useful among the stones of paths, where they can tolerate moderate foot traffic and

Thymus × citriodorus *'Aureus' (see* T. praecox arcticus)

scent the air when bruised. Fragrances range from savory thyme to lemon and caraway, depending upon the species. There are so many different kinds of thymes in a variety of flower and foliage colors, that it is difficult to select a few. *T. praecox arcticus* is an especially tough species and comes in varieties with red, pink, or white flowers. 'Hall's Woolly' (syn. *T. lanuginosus* 'Hall's Wooly') (Zone 5), woolly thyme, has gray hairy leaves and pale pink flowers. It needs a hotter, drier site with better drainage to prevent foliar rots. 'Pink Chintz' has salmon-pink flowers and is especially drought tolerant.

Related species: T. × citriodorus (Zone 5) is a bushy, lemon-scented hybrid. *T. × c.* 'Aureus' is a mounded creeper with attractive gold variegated foliage, and lavender flowers. *T. herba-barona* (Zone 4) has caraway-scented foliage.

Cultural information: Thymes are easily satisfied with a hot, dry location and well-drained, poor soil.

Willow, bearberry; see *Salix*

Woadwaxen; see *Genista*

CONIFERS

Arborvitae; see *Thuja*

Cedar, Japanese; see *Cryptomeria*

Cedar, white; see *Thuja*

Chamaecyparis obtusa
(kam-y-SIP-ar-is ob-TU-sa) **Hinoki false cypress** ○ ◑
Zone: 4
Native to: Japan
Uses: Rock garden, alpine meadow, scree
Characteristics: The dark green, fanlike foliage is composed of small scalelike needles. 'Golden Sprite' (10"×12" in 10 years) grows very slowly into a low, flat-topped golden mound, eventually becoming very broadly pyramidal. 'Hage' (15"×20" in 10 years) is a dense and widely pyramidal plant, also with a slow growth rate. 'Rigid Dwarf' (Zone 5, 25"×15" in 10 years) has very dark green foliage and an upright habit of growth.
Related species: C. *pisifera* 'Tsukumo' (Zone 4, 15"×20" in 10 years) is a very slow-growing cultivar, becoming wider than high, with fine-textured, dark green foliage.
Cultural information: The false cypresses are easily satisfied with almost any well-drained acid soil.

Cryptomeria japonica
(kryp-toh-MER-ee-a   ja-PON-y-ca) **Japanese cedar** ○ ◑
Zone: 6
Native to: Japan
Uses: Rock garden, alpine meadow, scree
Characteristics: Even the dwarf, compact varieties have coarse textured foliage. 'Tansu' (18"×24" in 10 years) has relatively fine-textured, light green foliage. It develops into a broad cone shape. 'Vilmoriniana' (12"×12" in 10 years) is an old and popular dwarf conifer that grows into a dense spherical mound, with foliage that turns reddish purple in winter. 'Compressa' is a similar cultivar.
Cultural information: Japanese cedars are easily grown in an acid, well-drained soil. They should be protected from winter sun and wind in harsh climates.

Chamaecyparis obtusa *'Golden Sprite'*

Cryptomeria japonica *'Compressa'*

Juniperus communis
'Compressa'

Picea glauca 'Alberta Globe'

Pinus mugo

Cypress, Hinoki false; see ***Chamaecyparis***

Douglas fir; see ***Pseudotsuga***

False cypress, Hinoki; see ***Chamaecyparis***

Fir, Douglas; see ***Pseudotsuga***

Hemlock; see ***Tsuga***

Hinoki false cypress; see ***Chamaecyparis***

Japanese cedar; see ***Cryptomeria***

Juniper; see ***Juniperus***

Juniperus communis (jew-NI-pir-us com-MEW-nis) **juniper** ○ ◑

Zone: 5

Native to: Europe, Asia, N. America

Uses: Rock garden, alpine meadow, wall, scree, trough

Characteristics: J. communis is a confusingly variable species with different forms ranging from small upright trees to low spreading shrubs. The foliage is composed of small, light blue-green prickly needles. 'Echiniformis' (6"×10" in 10 years) is a compact, squat, but rounded mound of blue-gray foliage. 'Compressa' (Zone 6, 18"×4" in 10 years) is one of the most useful and popular rock garden conifers providing upright exclamation points. It forms a tight, narrow, pointed spike. In harsh climates, locate away from strong winter sun and wind.

Related species: J. procumbens 'Nana' (Japan, Zone 5, 12"×30" in 10 years), with a low spreading habit, has been a popular plant for many years. It will creep over and around rocks and hang down over walls, but is too vigorous for small rock gardens. *J. squamata* 'Blue Star' (Zone 4, 18"×36" in 10 years) has a low spreading habit with engaging steel blue foliage. From above, the plant has the shape of a star. Requires full sun.

Cultural information: Junipers have the well-earned reputation of growing in poor, dry soils in hot locations where other plants will not. Reasonable drainage and sun seem to be the major requirements, although some will take partial shade.

Picea glauca (PY-see-a GLAW-ka) **spruce** ○ ◑

Zone: 2

Native to: N. America

Uses: Rock garden, alpine meadow, scree

Characteristics: The spruces have short, sharp, pointed needles. There are many dwarf forms from which to choose. *P. g.* 'Conica' is the ubiquitous dwarf Alberta spruce, which is sold at every nursery and garden center. While it will not become tree sized, many old specimens over 8 feet can be found in gardens, which demonstrates its unsuitability for rock gardens. 'Pixie' (Zone 3, 18"×12" in 10 years) has a similar conical shape and light green foliage, with a more desirable, slow rate of growth. 'Alberta Globe' (12"×18" in 10 years) also grows very slowly, but with a rounded habit and the characteristic light green needles.

Related species: P. abies 'Weiss' (18"×30" in 10 years) makes a tight, globe-shaped plant with very dark green foliage. *P. orientalis* 'Barnes Broom' (Zone 5, 15"×20" in 10 years) has quite short, very dark green needles and grows into a neatly uniform flattened globe. *P. pungens* 'St. Mary's Broom' (Zone 3, 8"×18" in 10 years) has beautiful blue needles and is one of the slowest growing blue spruces, forming a wide low mound.

Cultural information: Dwarf spruces grow best in a moist, well-drained soil of moderate fertility, which has been enriched with organic matter. Watch for spider mite infestations in hot summer weather.

Pine; see *Pinus*

Pinus mugo (PY-nus MEW-goh) **pine** ○
Zone: 2
Native to: C. and S. Europe
Uses: Rock garden, alpine meadow, scree
Characteristics: Pines have long needles in clusters of two to five. The mugo pines are generally low and mounded, never attaining tree status. Degree of vigor varies from one variety to another. 'Gnom' (20"×36" in 10 years) makes a low dense mound.
Related species: P. parviflora 'Adcock's Dwarf' (Zone 4, 18"×15" in 10 years) is a compact dwarf blue-green mound of slow growth. *P. strobus* 'Horsford' (10"×10" in 10 years) is a choice dwarf form of the popular eastern white pine. Its soft blue-gray foliage makes a compact mound. *P. sylvestris* 'Beuvronensis' (18"×36" in 10 years) has short needles with a greenish blue cast. This old cultivar, from the late 1800s, makes a tight, broad plant. *P. s.* 'Hillside Creeper' (12"×36" in 10 years) has a markedly prostrate habit, hugging the ground with a dense mat of long, bright green needles, that take on a gold cast in winter. It is too vigorous for small rock gardens, but makes an excellent groundcover for an adjacent bank.
Cultural information: Pines are relatively tolerant of poor soil but require good drainage.

Pseudotsuga menziesii
(SOO-doh-soo-ga   men-ZEE-zee-i)
Douglas fir ○
Zone: 4

Native to: W. N. America
Uses: Rock garden, alpine meadow, scree
Characteristics: Douglas firs have soft, flat needles. 'Pumila' (18"×24" in 10 years) makes a dense, flat-topped plant with upright branches. It is somewhat wider than high.
Cultural information: Douglas firs will grow best in a moderately acid, moist and well-drained soil.

Spruce; see *Picea*

Thuja occidentalis (THEW-ya ok-sy-den-TAL-is) **arborvitae, white cedar** ○ ◑
Zone: 2
Native to: E. N. America
Uses: Rock garden, alpine meadow
Characteristics: Flat sprays of foliage with light green scale-like needles characterize arborvitae. 'Hetz Midget' (18"×18" in 10 years) makes a small, tight globe.
Cultural information: Arborvitaes prefer a moist, well-drained soil of moderate fertility.

Tsuga canadensis (SOO-ga ka-na-DEN-sis) **hemlock** ◑
Zone: 3
Native to: E. N. America
Uses: Rock garden, alpine meadow, trough
Characteristics: The hemlock is one of the most common landscape conifers in both sun and shade. Dwarf cultivars are very useful in rock gardens. 'Cole' ('Cole's Prostrate') (Zone 4, 4"×15" in 10 years) is a stiffly prostrate plant with arching branches that hold its foliage tight against the ground. The thick, arching central trunks are bare of foliage. 'Everitt

Golden' (Zone 3, 24"×18" in 10 years) has dense, golden, upright foliage with an overall pyramidal shape. 'Minuta' (8"×10" in 10 years) makes a tight, congested, irregular mound that is very slow growing. It has been known to produce cones and comes true from seed, which are both unusual events with dwarf conifers.
Cultural information: Moist, acid soils with good drainage are best for hemlocks. Dwarf types prefer partial shade.

White cedar; see *Thuja*

Top: Pseudotsuga menziesii 'Compacta'

Middle: Thuja occidentalis 'Hetz Midget'

Bottom: Tsuga canadensis 'Cole's Prostrate'

PESTS AND DISEASES

Rock garden plants are relatively free of pests and diseases compared to other garden plants. When problems do occur, they are usually isolated and can be controlled by the simple methods discussed here. Chemical sprays are rarely necessary and may do more harm than good by killing off the beneficial insects and mites that prey on pests and they also pose a risk to the person using them.

Most problems with rock garden plants are caused by the stress of adapting to the heat and humidity of cultivation at low elevations. Many of these problems can be solved by correcting soil drainage and air circulation, or providing shade to reduce heat.

PESTS

Slugs and Snails

Slugs are soft, sausage-shaped and covered with thick, viscous slime but have no shell. They vary in size and range in color from light tan to black, sometimes with spots, depending on type. During the day they hide in cool, moist spots under stones, rotten wood, mulch, foliage and in the soil. At night and on rainy days, they come out to feed, preferring soft plant growth and showing a definite preference for certain kinds of plants. Dried slime trails on chewed foliage and on the ground are indications that they have been feeding on your plants. Snails are able to live in drier habitats because they can withdraw into their shells. Most gardeners would agree that slugs are the worse of the two pests, particularly in the East. Snails are a serious problem in California.

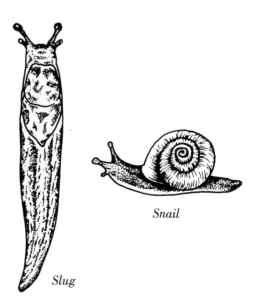

Snail

Slug

Control: The most popular way to control slugs is to set out shallow dishes of beer to which the slugs are irresistibly attracted. They crawl in and drown. You can also set moist rotten boards out and they will hide under them. Lift the board and collect them the next day. One of the most effective controls is to go out at night with a flashlight, find them at work and kill them. Snails should be picked and crushed whenever found.

Slugs prefer moist, clay soils and dislike dry, sandy ones. The open, dry conditions of many rock gardens tend to discourage them. Place a ring of sand around susceptible plants; it is difficult for slugs to crawl on sand.

Aphids

Aphids are small, green, reddish, white, clear or black pear-shaped insects. These pests, which tend to multiply rapidly, are found clustered along stems, under leaves and on flower buds. They prefer succulent new growth from which they suck plant juices. Aphids secrete a sticky, sugary substance called "honeydew" and deposit it on leaves and stems. The honeydew attracts ants and can provide an ideal environment for a harmless, but unsightly, black sooty mold.

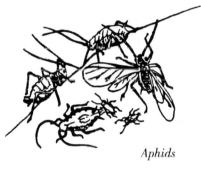

Aphids

Control: You can easily control aphids by spraying with insecticidal soap or superior oil, or by crushing them. Repeat treatments are often necessary, particularly in spring.

Scale

These sucking insects cling to branches and are protected by a scalelike shell that can vary in size, depending on the species. Usually found on woody plants outdoors, scale often goes unnoticed since the scales appear to blend with the bark.

Control: Once the shell has formed, they are difficult to kill, but during the active stage in spring, the "crawlers" are vulnerable to a spray of insecticidal soap or superior oil. At other seasons the scale can be rubbed off by hand. You can also apply a dormant oil spray to woody plants in early spring before buds break. The oil smothers the insects.

Mites

Mites are so tiny they are difficult to see without a magnifying glass. They are usually found on the underside of leaves where they feed by sucking. The first evidence of mites is tiny, light-colored speckles where they have destroyed the chlorophyll in the leaf. You may also find tiny spider webs close to the stem. Hot, dry weather encourages mite populations to proliferate.

Control: Fortunately, you can easily control mites by spraying with insecticidal soap. Be sure to wet the underside of the leaves completely. Repeat the treatments weekly to kill successive generations before they can lay eggs. Two to three applications should be adequate.

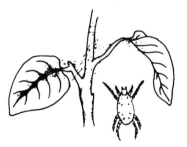

Spider mite

Red spider mite

Caterpillars

The larvae of moths and butterflies, caterpillars eat leaves of a variety of plants. Like slugs, these critters can cause a lot of damage in a short time on a small plant.

Control: Handpicking is the easiest solution. Larger numbers can be controlled by spraying the foliage with *Bacillus thuringiensis* (Bt).

Sow Bugs

Sow bugs are small crustaceans related to lobsters and crabs, that are often found in groups in moist places under pots and rocks. They look like armadillos, are dark in color with many legs and when disturbed, roll up into balls. Sow bugs seldom eat foliage, but they do eat plant roots and cause damage to stems that is not often discernible to the casual observer.

Control: The best method is to collect and destroy them when found, and eliminate hiding places.

Mice and Voles

These small rodents may burrow and tunnel, especially around rocks. Mice and voles can eat roots and bulbs, especially during the winter. They are especially fond of crocuses and tulips.

Control: The liberal use of gravel mixed into the soil is a powerful deterrent. Plant daffodils, Siberian squill, glory-of-the-snow and snowdrops, which are not likely to be eaten.

Chipmunks

These little rodents are one of the most serious pests in walls and rock gardens, because they make their burrows among rocks and stones, excavating the soil out from behind walls. Chipmunks also eat bulbs and other plants. The burrows give access to mice and voles.

Control: Control using the same methods as for mice and voles. You can also trap them.

Squirrels

Fortunately, squirrels do not burrow, but they do dig, and have a fondness for crocus corms and shallowly planted tulips. They also eat the young foliage and blooms of such spring bulbs as crocus and tulips when they are hungry enough. They can be found in the greatest numbers around oaks and other nut trees that produce a natural source of food.

Control: One of the easiest means of reducing squirrel damage at certain seasons is to feed them with peanuts to attract them away from your plants. Place wire mesh over low plants. Squirrels can be trapped easily, but the population recovers rapidly.

Rabbits and Deer

These animals need little description. One bite can eliminate a small rock plant.

Control: Fencing is the best protection, but can be costly for deer. Chemical deterrents sprayed on foliage have various rates of success and must be repeated frequently. Rabbits are difficult to entice into a live animal trap in summer.

DISEASES

Various diseases, including leafspots and rots, may affect rock plants. Most of these can be prevented or controlled by reducing moisture with good drainage and air circulation. Because of the small size of many rock plant parts, these problems are often not noticed until a dead branch or area develops. The only solution is to remove the affected plant parts. If a plant dies, it is usually advisable not to plant a closely related variety in the same spot for a few years until the disease dies out.

Powdery Mildew

A whitish or grayish coating on leaves, stems and flower buds, mildew is encouraged by damp, close conditions with poor air circulation.

Control: Be careful to water only when the foliage will dry rapidly, in the morning, for example, and avoid wetting foliage whenever possible. Dusting with sulphur or a fungicide may reduce further infection.

Crown and Foliage Rot

Crown rot causes the whole plant to die once the fungus cuts off the sap flow from the roots to the leaves. Similar organisms can infect a branch or foliage and cause it to die. Tight-tufted or mounded plants are especially susceptible because they hold moisture in their centers. Woolly, gray foliage is likely to "melt out" in hot, muggy weather because the woolly foliage does not dry effectively.

Control: Air circulation and drainage are the most important means of preventing rot. You can even use a fan to keep air moving! Clean off any dead foliage and debris that could harbor moisture. Avoid crowding plants, and remove any signs of infection.

Phytophthora Wilt

This fungus disease, which leads to the death of branches and eventually the whole plant, infects rhododendrons and related plants and is common in the nursery trade. Wilting of foliage (and flowers if in bloom) is the main symptom. Also, look for black staining under the bark. Wilting may occur a month or two after planting an infected nursery plant.

Control: Since this is a soil-borne disease, another rhododendron should not be planted in the same place unless all of the surrounding soil is replaced. During winter, remove all mulch from the area to encourage the soil to freeze deeply and kill the fungus, which is not very winter hardy.

GARDENERS' MOST-ASKED QUESTIONS

Q. Rock gardening seems quite specialized—do I have to be a very experienced gardener to be a rock gardener?
A. Anyone can grow rock plants successfully even in the smallest spaces, which makes it an ideal hobby for many people. All you need is a basic knowledge of the plants' needs and a suitable place to grow them. Good soil drainage and air circulation are the most important requirements. Most rock garden plants can be grown in containers, called "troughs." Beginners should select the easiest kinds of rock garden plants, which are forgiving of less than perfect conditions. Many of the easiest kinds are highlighted in this book and are available from good nurseries and garden centers or by mail order.

Q. Why are dwarf plants grown in rock gardens?
A. The primary inspiration of the rock garden is the rocky landscape of the mountainous regions of the world, particularly at high altitudes above the tree line where severe climatic conditions naturally dwarf plants. In essence, a rock garden is a miniature landscape. Many of the dwarf plants that are grown in rock gardens are not compatible with more vigorous varieties that could overgrow them. Larger plants are often out of scale with the rocks, which may become obscured. The larger the rock garden area and its rocks, the larger the plants can be.

Q. Are rocks actually essential to a rock garden?
A. Big rocks are not important to the health of rock plants in a garden, but stone chips or gravel are essential. Unlike bare soil, rocks and gravel dry off rapidly, which helps prevent disease and rot. When gravel is mixed in the soil it improves drainage. Many people living in areas where rocks are not readily available do grow rock plants without the company of large stones.

Q. I live in an area with hot, humid summers. Can I still have a rock garden?
A. Absolutely. Many dwarf plants are adapted to such climates. However, you must choose those plants that will tolerate your climate, and place less emphasis on true alpines. Some plants for you to try are stone cress, flowering onions, thrift, candytuft, moss pink, pasque flower, stonecrop, hen and chickens, dwarf goldenrod and some of the speedwells. Also try dwarf varieties of broom, spirea, boxwood, thyme, juniper, false-cypress, Japanese cedar and bulbs. Soil drainage and air circulation are especially important in these climates.

Q. Do any rock garden plants grow in shade?
A. The primary consideration for choosing plants for the shady rock garden is that they be dwarf, so as not to obscure the rocks. Such woodland plants as European ginger, green-and-gold, dwarf crested iris, primrose, dwarf ferns and dwarf rhododendrons are good choices. Some sun-loving rock garden plants will also grow in light or partial shade.

Q. Which rock garden plants bloom in late summer and fall?
A. For late-summer and fall bloom in the rock garden, try alpine aster, late-flowering on-

ions, Carpathian bellflower, late-flowering pink (*Dianthus superbus longicalycinus*), gentian (*Gentiana septemfida*), St.-John's-wort, soapwort, many stonecrops, campion, goldenrod, fall-blooming crocuses, colchicum, heather, dwarf spirea and thyme.

Q. Which plants are best for growing between paving stones?

A. Low-growing plants with a tough constitution are best suited to growing among paving stones. Those with fragrant foliage scent the air when walked upon. Try pinks, Corsican mint and creeping thymes.

Q. Should I fertilize my rock garden as much as I fertilize other garden areas?

A. No. Most rock garden plants are adapted to harsh climates and poor soils. Heavy feeding causes them to grow too rapidly, lose their neat forms and increase their susceptibility to disease. The best way to feed is with small quantities of such organic materials as leaf mold and compost, from which the nutrients are slowly released as the plants need them.

Q. Can vegetables and bedding plants be included in the rock garden?

A. For best performance, vegetables and bedding plants need to be grown in high fertility soils, which is contrary to the needs of rock plants. Such herbs as lavender and thyme, however, are good choices, because they prefer a poor soil. Small or dwarf varieties of annuals are sometimes included in rock gardens, but they are too vigorous and weedy for most alpines and rock plants to compete with.

Q. How often should I water my rock garden?

A. As infrequently as possible. Excess water, whether it be in the soil or on the foliage, is a major contributor to ill health of rock plants. Water only when the soil is dry or when the plants are wilted in the morning. Even with enough water in the soil, plants often wilt during the heat of midday, but they recover quickly in the evening. When you water, be sure the water penetrates deeply into the soil to encourage deep roots and to provide a deep reserve of moisture.

Q. Is root competition as much of a problem in rock gardens as it is in other gardens?

A. Root competition, particularly from trees, can be a problem in a rock garden if the trees (or shrubs) are too close to the plants. In only two or three years, roots can grow into a new rock garden and rob it of water and nutrients. In some situations, the roots will dry out the soil within a few days of being watered. When trees must be planted near a rock garden, choose kinds with deep roots, such as oaks, and avoid those with shallow roots, such as maples.

Q. Where can I get rocks? What should I look for when choosing rocks?

A. While you can gather your own rocks, most properties do not have enough natural stone to build a rock garden, and the rocks are often too small. The easiest way to obtain stone is to buy it at a local quarry and have them deliver it. Good rock garden stone is somewhat water absorbent and neither too hard nor too soft. Limestone and sandstone are considered some of the best types, but many others can be used (see page 31). Part of the consideration is what appeals to you and what kind of stone will look best in your chosen setting. It should match any existing stone as closely as possible. Old field stone with a weathered surface is preferred over the harshness of freshly quarried stone, but it is not always available.

Please write or call for a free Burpee catalog:
W. Atlee Burpee & Co.
300 Park Avenue
Warminster, PA 18974
(215) 674-9633

RESOURCE GUIDE

For American Rock Garden Society membership information, write:

Secretary
ARGS
P. O. Box 67
Millwood, New York 10546

Books for Further Reading:

Correvon, Henry. *Rock Garden and Alpine Plants.* The Macmillan Co., New York: 1930.

Farrer, Reginald. *The English Rock Garden.* 2 volumes. Theophrastus, Little Comptom, RI: Reprint 1976.

Farrer, Reginald. *The Rock Garden.* T. C. and E. C. Jack Ltd. London: 1932.

Foerster, Karl. *Rock Gardens Through the Year.* Sterling Publishing Co., New York: 1987.

Foster, H. Lincoln. *Rock Gardening, A Guide to Growing Alpines and Other Wildflowers in the American Garden.* Sagapress/Timber Press, Portland, OR: Reprint 1982.

Foster, H. Lincoln and Laura Louise Foster. *Cuttings from a Rock Garden.* Atlantic Monthly Press, New York: 1990.

Klaber, Doretta. *Rock Garden Plants: New Ways to Use Them Around Your Home.* Henry Holt and Co., New York: 1959.

Kolaga, Walter A. *All about Rock Gardens and Plants.* Doubleday and Co., New York: 1966.

Ingwersen, Will. *Manual of Alpine Plants.* Sterling Publishing Co., New York: 1991.

Ingwersen, Will. *Alpines.* Sagapress/Timber Press, Portland, OR: 1991.

Schenk, George. *How to Plan, Establish and Maintain Rock Gardens.* A Sunset Book, Lane Publishing Co., Menlo Park, CA.: 1964, Tenth Printing 1971.

Thomas, Graham Stuart. *The Rock Garden and its Plants.* Sagapress/Timber Press. Portland, OR: 1989.

Wilder, Louise Beebe. *Pleasures and Problems of a Rock Garden.* Garden City Publishing Co., New York: 1937.

Mail Order Sources:

Dilworth Nursery
1200 Election Road
Oxford, PA 19363
(215) 932-0347
    Dwarf conifers.

Forestfarm
990 Tetherow Road
Williams, OR 97544-9599
(503) 846-6963
    Wide selection of all kinds of plants, including dwarf types. Catalog $3.00

Miniature Plant Kingdom
4125 Harrison Grade Rd.
Sebastopol, CA 95472
(707) 874-2233
    Dwarf plants, including conifers, shrubs, alpines and perennials. Catalog $2.00

Paw Paw Everlasting Label Co.
P.O. Box 93-WR
Paw Paw, MI 49079-0093
    metal labels

Rice Creek Gardens
1315 66th Ave. N.E.
Minneapolis, MN 55432
    Rock garden plants, alpines, dwarf conifers and rhododendrons. Catalog $2.00

Rock Spray Nursery, Inc.
Box 693
Truro, MA 02666
(508) 349-6769
    Heaths and heathers, and other dwarf ericaccous plants. Catalog $1.00

Rocky Mountain Rare Plants
P.O. Box 200483
Denver, CO. 80220
(303) 322-1410
    Seed of western native rock garden plants. Catalog $1.00

Siskiyou Rare Plant Nursery
2825 Cummings Road
Medford, OR 97501
(503) 772-6846
    Alpines and dwarf plants of all kinds for rock gardens. Catalog $2.00

Walt Nicke Co.
36 McLeod Lane
P.O. Box 433
Topsfield, MA 01983
(800) 822-4114
    Labels, tools and other garden supplies.

Wrightman Alpines
R. R. #3
Kerwood, Ontario,
Canada NOM 2BO
(519) 247-3751
    Rock garden and alpine plants. Catalog $1.00

THE USDA PLANT HARDINESS MAP OF THE UNITED STATES

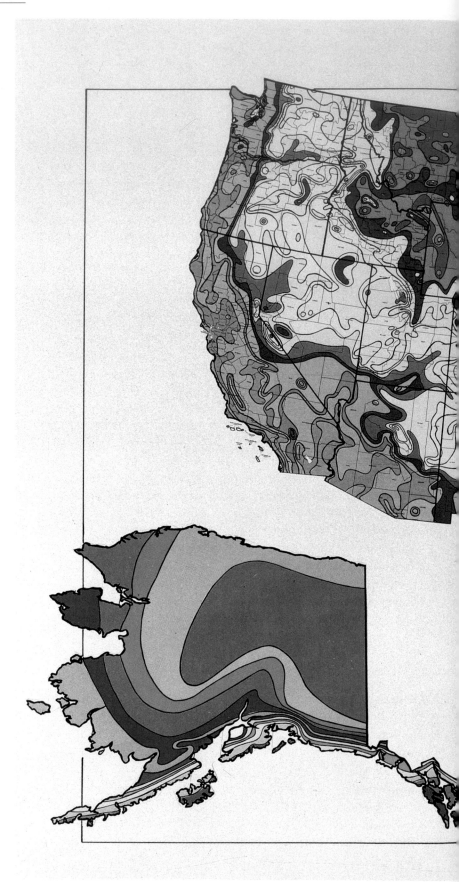

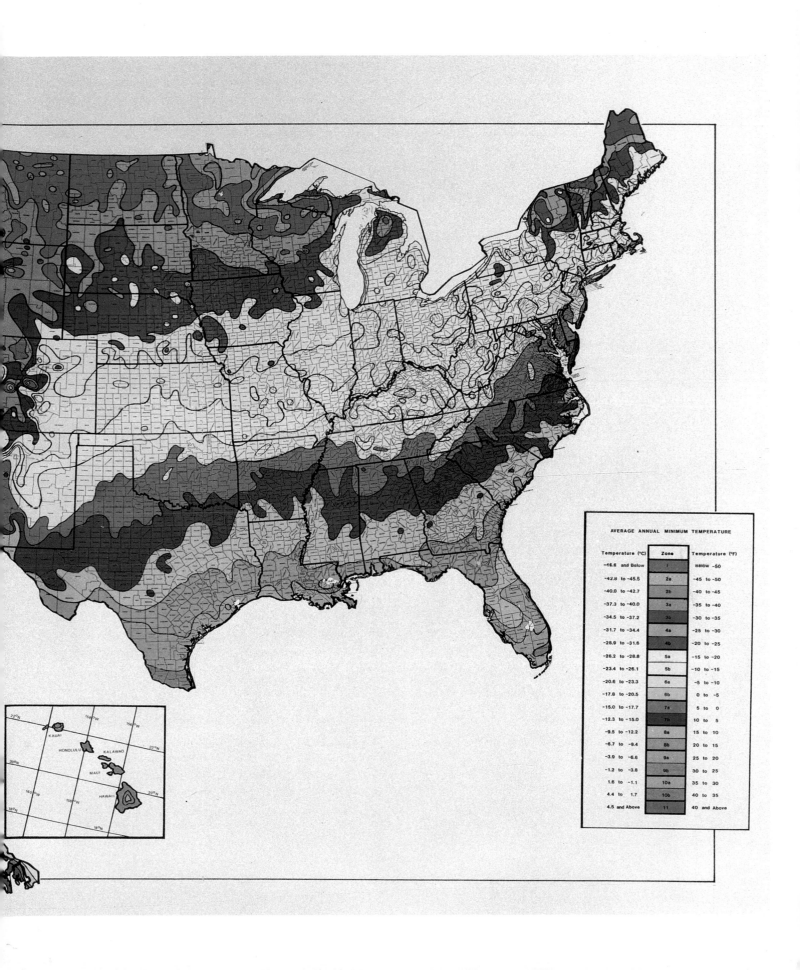

AVERAGE ANNUAL MINIMUM TEMPERATURE

Temperature (°C)	Zone	Temperature (°F)
-45.6 and Below	1	Below -50
-42.8 to -45.5	2a	-45 to -50
-40.0 to -42.7	2b	-40 to -45
-37.3 to -40.0	3a	-35 to -40
-34.5 to -37.2	3b	-30 to -35
-31.7 to -34.4	4a	-25 to -30
-28.9 to -31.6	4b	-20 to -25
-26.2 to -28.8	5a	-15 to -20
-23.4 to -26.1	5b	-10 to -15
-20.6 to -23.3	6a	-5 to -10
-17.8 to -20.5	6b	0 to -5
-15.0 to -17.7	7a	5 to 0
-12.3 to -15.0	7b	10 to 5
-9.5 to -12.2	8a	15 to 10
-6.7 to -9.4	8b	20 to 15
-3.9 to -6.6	9a	25 to 20
-1.2 to -3.8	9b	30 to 25
1.6 to -1.1	10a	35 to 30
4.4 to 1.7	10b	40 to 35
4.5 and Above	11	40 and Above

INDEX

(NOTE: Italized page numbers refer to captions)

Cut along dotted line.

Cut along dotted line.